Competition among Airlines

GW00401245

The third title, in the Thames Essay series, arising out of the Trade Policy Research Centre's programme of studies on Restrictions on Transactions in the International Market for Services, supervised by Brian Hindley, the Centre's Counsellor for Studies. The earlier titles were

Barriers to Trade in Banking and Financial Services
by Ingo Walter

Outlook for the Liberalisation of Maritime Transport
by Elliot Schrier, Ernest Nadel and Bertram Rifas

Other titles in the programme to be published as Thames Essays are provisionally entitled

Barriers to Trade in Insurance and Reinsurance
by Robert L. Carter and Gerard M. Dickinson

Protection of Property Rights in the Ideas Market
by Jennifer Skilbeck

European Shipping Policy towards Developing Countries
by Hans Böhme

The cartoon by Dick Locher, reproduced by permission of Tribune Media Services, on the front cover is taken from an issue of the *Chicago Tribune*, 1982. In this Thames Essay, Richard Pryke argues that de-regulation of international airlines will not lead to destructive competition, but will encourage a more streamlined and efficient industry.

Thames Essay No. 46

Competition among International Airlines

BY

Richard Pryke

Gower

Aldershot · Brookfield USA · Hong Kong · Singapore · Sydney

for the

TRADE POLICY RESEARCH CENTRE

London

First published 1987 by

Gower Publishing Company Limited, Gower House, Croft Road, Aldershot, Hampshire GU11 3HR, United Kingdom

Gower Publishing Company, Old Post Road, Brookfield, Vermont 05036, United States of America

Gower Publishing Australia, 85 Whiting Street, Artamon, New South Wales 2064, Australia

ISSN 0306-6991
ISBN 0566 05333 0

British Library Cataloguing-in-Publication Data
Pryke, Richard
    Competition among International Airlines.
    (Thames Essay No. 46)
    1. Aeronautics, Commercial 2. Competition
    I. Title II. Trade Policy Research Centre
    III. Series
    387.7'1   HE9777

Library of Congress Cataloging-in-Publication Data
Pryke, Richard
    Competition among International Airlines.
    (Thames Essay No. 46)
    1. Aeronautics, Commercial.
    2. Competition, International.
    3. Aeronautics, Commercial — Deregulation.
    4. Air Lines — Rates.
    I. Trade Policy Research Centre. II. Title.
    III. Series.
    HE9780.P79   1987   387.7'1   86-31877

Printed in the United Kingdom by
Biddles Ltd, Guildford, Surrey

Contents

Biographical Note

RICHARD PRYKE, a Senior Lecturer in Economics at the University of Liverpool, has taken a special interest in the economic performance of public enterprises in the United Kingdom. He is the author of *Public Enterprise in Practice: the British Experience of Nationalisation over Two Decades* (1971), and *The Nationalised Industries: Policies and Performance since 1968* (1981); and he is the co-author of *The Rail Problem* (1975).

After graduating from the University of Oxford in 1958, Dr Pryke later pursued his studies at the University of Illinois, in the United States, and then for three years he was engaged on research in the Department of Applied Economics at the University of Cambridge. In 1967, he took up a teaching appointment at the University of Liverpool, where he obtained his doctorate in 1972.

Dr Pryke worked in the research department of the Labour Party in 1958-60 and 1961-64. He was a Labour Party candidate in the British general elections of 1964 and 1966. In 1970-75 he was a member of various sub-committees of the Labour Party's national executive, including the public enterprise group, which planned the National Enterprise Board.

Preface

FOR five years discussions have been proceeding at inter-governmental level on what might be done about the liberalization of trade and investment in the services sector of the world economy. Initially, deliberations were got under way in the Organisation for Economic Cooperation and Development (OECD), where the governments of developed countries discuss economic issues of common interest. Soon after, the subject was taken up in the framework of the General Agreement on Tariffs and Trade (GATT), the instrument which governs the institutional environment of international trade among the market-oriented economies.

In neither forum was the subject entirely new. But the deliberations in both have acquired a new dimension, partly as a result of general pressures which reflect technological advances in the services sector, especially in transport and communications, and partly as a result of specific pressures which, in particular countries, reflect the 'internationalization' of the services sector in keeping with the integration of the world economy as whole.

Pursuing an interest which dates back to the early 1970s, the Trade Policy Research Centre embarked in 1981 on a major programme of studies on restrictions on transactions in the international market for services. The programme, supervised by Brian Hindley, the Centre's Counsellor for Studies, has been supported by a generous grant from the Ford Foundation in New York, with other grants from the

Rockefeller, Starr and American Express foundations, also in New York, from the German Marshall Fund in Washington and from the Nuffield, Esmée Fairbairn and Baring foundations in London.

The programme included a study on international civil aviation, which has been carried out by Richard Pryke, of the University of Liverpool. A first draft of the paper arising from the study was discussed at a meeting at Ditchley Park, near Oxford, on 29-31 October 1982 attended by senior airline executives, public officials and independent experts and chaired by Lord Marsh, a former Minister of Transport in the British Government. Lord Marsh summed up the discussion in 'Prospects for the Liberalisation of Civil Aviation', published in *The World Economy*, December 1982. Dr Pryke revised the draft in the light of discussion at the meeting, then developed the paper further and revised it again in the light of comments from civil aviation experts in North America and Western Europe. The final product is this Thames Essay.

Three factors have lately combined to focus considerable attention in the developed countries on the conduct of civil aviation affairs at domestic (or regional) and international levels. First, there has been the deregulation of domestic routes in the United States, which began in 1978. Second, there has been the impact of the recession, or rather the prolonged period of slow growth, on the finances of the airlines. Third, there has been the marked increase in public criticism of the present system of international civil aviation, based on bilateral agreements loosely related through a multilateral agreement.

These considerations have a bearing on the debate in the European Community on the Commission's proposals, advanced in March 1984, for achieving a greater degree of flexibility and competition with respect to air fares, route capacity and market access. The proposals drew responses from the Association of European Airlines (AEA), the European Civil Aviation Conference (ECAC) and the International Air Transport Association (IATA) and a report was prepared in the Community's Parliament. Reflecting dissatisfaction with the responses, the Commissioner for Transport, Mr Stanley Clinton Davis, declared in the Autumn of 1985 that governments and airlines would be taken to the Community's Court of Justice if they did not take action by June 1986 to liberalize intra-Community civil aviation in conformity with the competition provisions of the Treaty of Rome. Pressure for action increased when in the spring of this year, the Court of Justice ruled, in the *Nouvelles Frontières* case, that civil aviation in the Community is subject to the Community's competition provisions.

In advocating its proposals for liberalizing civil aviation in the European Community, the Commission has referred, *inter alia*, to public dissatisfaction with the current arrangements. European airlines have replied that they always try to meet the requirements of customers and point to many innovations. But the public will always look for lower prices and better service, it is argued, and therefore public opinion is not a sufficiently objective yardstick with which to measure airline efficiency.

This argument reveals a major political problem for the airlines. One consequence of the present structure of international civil aviation, based on bilateral agreements, is that there is very little net trade in airline services. It is as if Hong Kong were permitted to export clothing only to the extent that she imports clothing. The international civil aviation system, as it stands at present, leads to a very high level of protection against imports.

In many other industries a new supplier is free to enter any part of the market if it believes that it can compete profitably with those already established there. Thus purchasers of the products of an industry are not entirely dependent on assurances of goodwill from established suppliers. Freedom of entry and competition provide them with another, and possibly a more satisfactory, form of assurance that the industry's products are being sold at prices which are the lowest possible consistent with quality.

A regulated industry cannot offer this assurance. It relies on the political power behind the regulatory system to maintain the *status quo*. But in representative democracies the availability of such power depends heavily on the ability of producers in the industry to persuade the public at large that they, the producers, are not exploiting their position. If the *prima facie* evidence of exploitation becomes great, the regulated structure is vulnerable. Such is the case with the provision of airline services in Western Europe.

As usual, it has to be stressed that the views expressed in this Thames Essay do not necessarily represent those of members of the Council or those of the staff and associates of the Trade Policy Research Centre which, having general terms of reference, does not represent a consensus of opinion on any particular issue. The purpose of the Centre is to promote independent analysis and public discussion of international economic policy issues.

HUGH CORBET
Director
Trade Policy Research Centre

London
August 1986

Chapter 1

Towards a Better Understanding of Civil Aviation

UNTIL a few years ago the international airlines provided a service which, if not silent, was one about which silence prevailed. Academic and polemical studies had appeared from time to time, usually critical in nature, but they served only to emphasize rather than to disturb the monopolistic calm that reigned. The situation today has changed almost beyond recognition. Controversy rages about what is happening in the United States, where domestic civil aviation has been de-regulated, and loud claims and counter-claims are made about the supposed virtues and alleged evils of greater competition, whether realized or potential, among the international airlines.

With one or two exceptions the major international airlines are strongly opposed to any loosening of the restrictive arrangements under which international civil aviation is conducted and would like, if possible, to return to the *status quo ante* in which greater discipline prevailed. This point of view has been forcefully expressed by Pierre Giraudet, as Chairman of Air France:

'International air transport is obviously in a bad way...

Bad ... because of the deregulation backed by various governments which, whether from *naïveté* or from demagogy, wished to believe that free-for-all competition would lead to miracles of traffic growth and of cost decreases; alas, by destroying the necessary minimum organization of the market, this pseudo-consumerism has led to an industry-wide recession, to the generalized

deficits of the international carriers (and to the total
disappearance of some of them), and finally to a decrease
of supply in quantity and quality on the most deregulated
markets.'[1]

This was written when the industry was experiencing financial
problems in the early 1980s. Other international airlines tend
to express their views in a more moderate manner, but they,
too, generally believe that liberalization is synonymous with
disaster. Nevertheless, many airlines would like to enjoy greater
freedom and flexibility in their operations without the
concomitant disadvantage (from their point of view) of having
to face greater competition.

Some of the critics of the existing situation in international
civil aviation regard the case in favour of liberalization as being
equally overwhelming. They base their indictment of regulation
on comparisons which appear to show that standard air fares
are much lower in the United States, where de-regulation has
taken place, than they are in Western Europe, where it has
not. In the United Kingdom, the Civil Aviation Authority
(CAA) has shown, however, that this comparison is not as
favourable to the United States as is generally believed.
According to the CAA:

'A comprehensive comparison of normal fares on routes
with regular jet service from New York, Atlanta and
London, reveals that [in October 1982]:

(i) On almost every route out of Atlanta, and on
many of the smaller routes out of New York, normal
fares have risen at a higher rate than costs since de-
regulation.

(ii) On such routes the typical normal fare is now
only 10-15 per cent less than the lowest normal fare
from London (Eurobudget) for the same distance at
the current exchange rate.

(iii) There are a significant number of routes,
particularly the longer ones, out of New York on
which the lowest available normal fare [but not the
general level of normal fares charged by other

carriers] has fallen considerably in real terms. On these routes [the lowest normal] fares are, in some cases, as low as one third of the lowest normal fare for routes of the same distance from London.'[2]

Because only about one fifth of all passengers on domestic airline services in the United States now pay the standard fare, the CAA study does not mean that the average revenue per passenger-mile, or 'yield', is nearly as high in the United States as it is in Western Europe.[3] Indeed, the CAA study goes on to show, among other things, that the yield per passenger-mile is far higher on services within Western Europe than it is on services provided by Delta, which is a typical major American carrier that operates out of Atlanta. Unfortunately, such comparisons of costs are open to the objection that the cost of fuel, and some other inputs, is much greater in Western Europe than in the United States.

What is called for, and what this study aims to provide, is a thorough and objective examination of the arguments and evidence for and against the liberalization of international civil aviation.[4] Denunciations of de-regulation, in which the airlines engage, only serve to generate heat, while crude comparisons between fares, which are the stock-in-trade of those who advocate more open competition, do not produce compelling evidence. The next chapter looks at the international airline system, Chapter 3 examines the American experience since de-regulation and in Chapter 4 the theoretical arguments in favour of regulation are considered, although there is no reason why the theoretical chapter should not be read first.

NOTES AND REFERENCES

1. Pierre Giraudet, 'The Challenge to Air France', Skyways, Bombay, March 1983.

2. *A Comparison Between European and United States Fares*, CAA Paper 83006 (London: Civil Aviation Authority, 1983) pp. 20, 23 and 27.

3. A *passenger-mile* is a passenger moved over a mile. The number

of passenger-miles is obtained for each flight between airports by multiplying the number of passengers by the distance. A *seat-mile* is a seat moved over a mile and the number is obtained in the same way as for passenger-miles. The corresponding measures when freight is included are the load tonne-mile and the capacity tonne-mile. A *load tonne-mile* is one tonne of load — whether in the form of passengers, freight or a combination of the two — carried for a distance of one mile. A *capacity tonne-mile* is one tonne of capacity for the transport of passengers and/or freight moved over a distance of one mile. The *load-factor* is the number of load tonne-miles expressed as a percentage of the number of capacity tonne-miles. The *passenger load-factor* is the number of passenger-miles as a percentage of the number of seat-miles.

4. What will not be discussed here is the question of the qualitative regulation of the aviation industry in the interests of safety. It will be implicitly assumed that such regulations will continue and will remain effective. The American experience of de-regulation, analysed in Chapter 3, suggests that accidents do not increase when controls over entry and fares are removed but safety regulations remain in force.

Chapter 2

Critique of the International Airline System

THIS chapter is a critique of the international airline system. It begins with an examination of the international agreements and arrangements which limit the freedom of scheduled airlines to operate where they choose, to determine how much capacity they will provide and to decide what fares they will charge. The chapter then goes on to look at the way in which, largely due to the impetus given by the charter carriers, the industry has become less restrictive.

Nevertheless, as the following sections will show, competition has not increased to the point where fares are related at all closely to costs. There are wide and persistent differences in profitability between regions, within regions between airlines, within at least one region — Europe — between short-haul and long-haul routes and between individual routes, where the variation in financial performance must be huge. Carriers earn abnormally high profits in some places which are then used to meet losses elsewhere. It appears that the airlines tend to over-charge those passengers who buy standard full-fare tickets and often under-charge those who buy discount tickets. The latter part of the chapter contains an examination of unit costs and it is shown that, even after adjustment to allow for distorting factors, there are large variations from one part of the industry to another. Moreover, there is reason to believe that pilots, and some other groups as well, receive excessively high pay.

Before embarking on the examination of the international airline system, it may be useful to provide some background information on the way in which the industry's output, productivity and fares have been changing. Over the past decade, civil aviation has been expanding very rapidly. Between 1973 and 1983, the volume of traffic on international scheduled services, as measured by the number of passenger miles, increased by 7.9 per cent per annum, which meant that it more than doubled in these ten years. In comparison, gross domestic product (GDP) at constant prices of the industrialized market economies increased by only 2.2 per cent per annum.[1]

One reason why airline traffic grew faster than the GDP is that as incomes rise a more than proportionate amount of the increased income is spent on travel; in other words, the income elasticity of demand for travel is high. A second explanation for the huge increase in traffic is that the industry has, partly because of the rapid technological progress of the aircraft manufacturers, made large gains in productivity. The scheduled airlines had an increase of 41 per cent in tonne-miles per aircraft over the period 1972-82 and there was a rise of 68 per cent (or 5.3 per cent per annum) in the number of tonne-miles per worker. This was much greater than the general increase in productivity; GDP per worker in the industrialized market economies only rose by 1.6 per cent a year.

One result of the exceptionally rapid growth of productivity in the airline industry is that air fares have increased much less than the general level of prices. Between 1972 and 1982 the revenue per passenger-mile from all scheduled traffic rose by 7 per cent per annum compared with an increase of 13 per cent a year in the cost of living in the industrialized market economies in the same period. This substantial reduction in air fares in real terms has obviously contributed to the increase in the volume of traffic.[2]

In spite of the rapid expansion of the airline industry, it is still small when measured either by the inputs it employs or by the output it provides. In 1982, the international scheduled airlines had about 1 million employees, excluding the Soviet Union and the People's Republic of China. This is not very much greater than the number once employed by the British Transport Commission, which was responsible for British Rail and a major part of the public transport network in the United Kingdom. Moreover, in 1983 the number of passenger-miles on international scheduled air services was only fifteen times greater than that on British Rail and the London Underground. The total volume of world air traffic in 1983 was, indeed, no greater than the number of passenger-miles travelled by public and private transport in Great Britain.[3]

Bilateral Agreements and IATA

Largely due to British opposition, the international conference at Chicago in 1944 failed to produce a multinational agreement providing certain 'freedoms' of the air. As a result, countries have negotiated bilaterally for the exchange of commercial rights. Under these bilateral agreements, their aircraft were permitted to operate scheduled services between the two countries at either end of the route involved and so exercise what are known as the third and fourth freedoms of the air. (The first freedom is the privilege of flying over a country without landing and the second that of landing for such purposes as refuelling, but not to pick up or set down traffic.) Sometimes the bilateral agreements permitted passengers to be picked up or set down *en route* and thereby included what are known as fifth-freedom rights. The amount of fifth-freedom traffic is, to this day, extremely limited and it probably constitutes less than 5 per cent of all traffic passing between the (non-Warsaw Pact) countries that belong to the European Civil Aviation Conference (ECAC). This is due not only to the absence of fifth-freedom rights but also to lack of interest on the part of the airlines in this freedom because intermediate stops make services less attractive.[4]

In some cases the bilateral agreements specify that each of the parties is to be represented by a single airline. A survey in 1982 revealed that it was laid down in about 30 per cent of the arrangements between the ECAC countries that there should be only one national airline per country per route. Even when the bilateral agreements do not impose such restrictions, it is the policy of most governments that there should be only one national airline on each route and they object strongly if the other country wants to have more than one carrier. On only 2 per cent of the routes between the ECAC countries were there two or more national operators per country. At the beginning of 1985, the only European routes on which more than one carrier operated were eight routes from London. On these eight routes, British Caledonian or some other carrier operated services from Gatwick in addition to the services operated by British Airways from Heathrow. Outside Western Europe, routes where there are more than two principal operators are equally few and far between, and the United States is the only country besides the United Kingdom that has made any attempt to secure 'dual designation'.

Most bilateral agreements make some provision for the control of capacity. The two main forms of control are (i) the pre-determination of capacity and (ii) an *ex post* review of the position. Thirty per cent of the agreements between the ECAC countries provide for control through pre-determination and 60 per cent provide for an *ex post* review. In many cases these reviews seem to have little effect, but this does not mean that there are no restrictions on capacity. On most routes there are commercial arrangements for the control of capacity between the principal airlines which, because they involve some element of revenue sharing, are known as pooling agreements. The survey in 1982 showed that such agreement covered 75-85 per cent of the tonne miles on flights between the ECAC countries, much of the remaining work being on routes where only one airline operates. About 70 per cent of the pooling agreements involved joint decisions on the frequencies to be operated and around 25 per cent involved the forward planning of capacity, load factors and schedule frequency for periods of longer than twelve months.

The final important feature of the agreements on civil aviation is a commitment to price-setting. The bilateral treaties usually declare that the airlines should, subject to government approval, reach agreement on their air fares; and it is often stated that the price-setting machinery of the International Air Transport Association (IATA) shall, wherever possible, be used. This is repeated in, and reinforced by, the international agreement for the establishment of prices for scheduled services, to which 15 of the 22 countries belonging to ECAC are signatories. IATA was established in 1945 in order that prices might be set on a comprehensive basis. Because competitive price-setting had been virtually ruled out at the Chicago Conference, this was necessary. One reason was that in the United States the regulatory authority — the (now defunct) Civil Aeronautics Board (CAB) — did not have any jurisdiction over fares submitted by individual carriers, but was empowered to grant anti-trust immunity for agreements among carriers.[5] The main reason for the establishment of a system of comprehensive fare setting, however, was to prevent the fares on one route being undercut by the fares on another. It was a basic principle of the IATA fare structure that it must not be cheaper to travel from A to C via B than to fly directly from A to C.

Until 1979, IATA had been divided into three geographical areas for the purpose of price-setting, with the agreement of all the voting airlines being necessary before a fare scheme for a particular area could come into effect. This meant that no airline had to accept fares that were too low to cover its costs. During 1979, IATA was split into eleven sub-areas and agreements on fares within or between sub-areas can now take effect provided that all the participating airlines concur and that no more than four, or 19.9 per cent, of the carriers in the area object. If no general agreement can be reached, the airlines involved in operating a route are permitted to agree their fares bilaterally, provided a majority of the airlines in the relevant area do not vote against the suggested scheme. In practice, most fares within Western Europe, which is a sub-area, continue to be fixed collectively, but it appears that on a small but growing proportion of the routes they are set on a bilateral basis. Moreover, so long as they can agree, the third-freedom and fourth-freedom carriers on a route are allowed to introduce so-called 'innovative' fares and airlines on other routes are permitted to respond. These moves away from multilateralism mean that IATA is somewhat less restrictive than it used to be.

IATA has never functioned like a cartel in which excessive profits were earned. On the contrary, profits have been abnormally low. During the years 1955-65, for example, the international airlines in IATA earned an average operating return of 3 per cent, as against a return on private industrial investments of 6-8 per cent or even more in that period.[6] Most airlines were in state ownership. They had no incentive to maximize profits and few were under pressure to do much more than break even. Moreover, a policy of crude profit maximization would ultimately have led to the withdrawal of the privileges and protection which governments had conferred. These 'flag-carrying' airlines, whether in public or private ownership, came to see their role as the providers of services that were frequent, extensive and — because there were plenty of spare seats available — dependable. In this way, the airlines provided themselves with a *raison d'être*; and they were able to satisfy politicians and airline users that they were providing something in return for the exclusive rights they possessed and the high prices they often charged. Because services were frequent, extensive and dependable, the load factor tended to be very low. Over the five-year period 1968-72 it averaged little more than 50 per cent on international services. Furthermore, although the general level of fares was not excessive (given the general level of costs), some fares were much too high and others much too low, resulting in a welter of cross-subsidization.

CHARTER COMPETITION

The scheduled airline system that existed from the end of World War II until the mid-1970s has, during the period since then, been modified but not transformed. Except for the North Atlantic and, now, some arrangements between the United Kingdom and continental countries, the terms of bilateral agreements remain much the same and, as shown, are usually highly restrictive. But the system of price fixing through IATA has partly broken down. As a result, fare structures have tended to become more flexible and there is now some price competition within the scheduled network. The impetus for this change was provided from outside by the charter carriers who began by meeting the air transport requirements of holiday tour operators. Under the Chicago Convention non-scheduled services of this type were treated in a somewhat more liberal fashion than scheduled operations. Whereas scheduled services could not be provided without the special permission of the countries involved, non-scheduled services could be operated subject to any conditions that were imposed by the relevant countries.

This was a fine distinction which did not for some time have much practical significance. But in the mid-1950s the countries belonging to ECAC agreed that flights for inclusive holiday tours were to be regarded as permissible, non-scheduled work. Although the member countries could, and in some cases did, impose restrictions, there was a rapid growth in inclusive tour operations within Western Europe. During the mid-1970s, charter operators started to provide 'throw away' inclusive tours, where the accommodation was primitive and the customer was, in reality, purchasing pure transport. Certain governments, including those of Spain and Greece, have not prevented charters of this type, but others have largely stopped them by establishing a minimum fare, which is strictly enforced.

The North Atlantic was another place where non-scheduled traffic became important because of the liberalization of charter operations which took place during the first half of the 1960s.

It became possible for some organization or 'affinity', which was not supposed to have travel as its primary purpose, to charter aircraft and sell seats to its members. Bogus organizations were established and from 1973 'affinity'-group charters were replaced by advanced-booking charters.

By the early 1970s the charter carriers accounted for a significant part of the total market. In 1972 these non-scheduled airlines carried 15 per cent of all international traffic, as measured by load tonne-miles (and the non-scheduled work of the scheduled airlines represented a further 13 per cent). The scheduled operators found it difficult to compete with the charter concerns because their costs were so much higher, at least on their scheduled services. In the United Kingdom in 1977, the CAA and British Airways made a joint study, known as Cascade, to determine why expenditure by British Airways was greater than that of charter operators on three representative routes in Western Europe. It found that British Airways would have had costs per passenger that were 110-175 per cent higher than those of the charter firms if it had transported their traffic in the same way that it carried its own passengers.[7] Although the seasonal variation was greater for charter passengers and this made them more expensive to carry, British Airways incurred considerable expense by providing higher standards of comfort and service, its aircraft had a lower utilization and its load factor was inferior. Tour operators using charter carriers managed to fill a very high proportion of the seats available on their aircraft by adjusting their prices and slotting passengers into vacant seats.[8] A similar study of the Dutch carrier KLM showed that, during 1979-80, its adjusted costs were 85-115 per cent greater than those of a charter concern which operated on the same Mediterranean route.

EFFECTS AND EXTENT OF COMPETITION

The scheduled airlines ultimately responded to the growth in charter traffic by introducing fares that were more competitive and, because of their high costs, they were forced to think of ways in which passengers on discount fares could be carried more cheaply. According to Douglas Adkins and his colleagues at the CAB in the United States,

'The growth of charter service [on the North Atlantic] during the 1960s and early 1970s led to the introduction of a number of new scheduled fare categories designed to combat it. Group-inclusive tour fares (GITs) were offered in 1967, excursion fares with 22-29 to 45 day minimum-stay requirements first appeared in 1970 and advance purchase excursions (Apex) were introduced in 1974.'[9]

Competition intensified during 1977 when the IATA carriers failed to reach agreement on fares, and the Laker Skytrain service was inaugurated at a charter-competitive price. As a result, the existing scheduled airline operators introduced much lower discount fares between London and New York, including 'standby' and Super Apex, which, for the first time, more or less matched those of the charter firms. The year 1977 also saw the first of the agreements that have made the North Atlantic services more competitive by establishing extra routes and enabling new American carriers, which do not belong to IATA, to enter the market. These carriers include airlines which had previously been largely confined to American domestic operations, like Delta, carriers that had been exclusively engaged in charter work, such as World, and new carriers, as represented by People Express. The last began operating across the Atlantic in 1983 and is trying to become a large low-fare carrier. If it succeeds, it will take over the role that Laker Airways relinquished when it went bankrupt in 1982.

In some ways the increase in competition has led to greater efficiency on the North Atlantic routes. In order to reduce their costs and compete with the charter operators, the scheduled airlines began, during the early 1960s, to sell off blocks of seats to firms organizing package tours. In this way they could reduce reservation and marketing costs and increase the passenger load factor. Apex fares were another cost-cutting

development. The old excursion fares, which on the North
Atlantic have largely been replaced by Apex fares, were simply
a way of providing a discount. But when there are Apex fares,
the number of seats for those travelling on this type of ticket
is fixed in advance, only a limited number of seats are made
available at peak times and control is exercised to ensure that
the correct number of seats have been set aside. As a result
of Apex and 'standby' tickets, the passenger load factor on
the North Atlantic services rose from 58 per cent in 1973 to
68 per cent in 1983. The passenger load factor in the North
Atlantic region is higher than for any other region; on
international services in the rest of the world it averaged 60
per cent in 1983.[10]

The North Atlantic accounts for about a quarter of all
passenger-miles flown on international services and is the most
important area where there is a substantial degree of
competition. Nevertheless, even here an attempt has been
made to establish minimum fares and prices were increased
once Laker Airways had ceased to be a threat. The presence
or absence of Apex fares provides some indication of whether,
because of greater competition, rates have become flexible and
of whether the airlines are under any real pressure to reduce
their fares and cut their costs. Apex fares have been introduced
on most international routes in North America and across the
Pacific and mid-Atlantic. Fares of this type have also been
introduced to a substantial degree on West European internal
services, on the routes from North America to Central America
and the Caribbean and on the services from South America
to other parts of the Western Hemisphere. They have been
introduced as well on some routes between Western Europe
and the Far East and the Pacific. A survey by the International
Civil Aviation Organization (ICAO) suggests that in the
autumn of 1982 there were Apex or other deep-discount fares
on 28 per cent of all routes, although the figure has probably
increased since then.[11]

It would be wrong though to regard all these routes as truly
competitive. Deep-discount fares have often been introduced

as a pre-emptive device in order to make it more difficult for charter operators to compete and to reduce the risk that governments will license more operators. It is true, however, that fares have become more flexible and that, when over-capacity emerged during 1980-82, there was selective price cutting on a large number of routes. Although fares were generally maintained at the levels which the airlines had jointly established, spare seats were disposed off at knock-down prices through 'bucket' shops. IATA is now trying to prevent this practice.

CONTINUING WEAKNESSES OF THE SYSTEM

That the international airline industry has not become truly competitive is shown by the widespread and indeed well-nigh universal failure to relate fares to costs or to adjust the amount of capacity to the quantity of traffic. As will become evident, fares are greatly above costs in some places, while in others they are greatly below. Not only do these discrepancies exist but they also persist. If competition were stronger and less restricted, differences in profitability would be unlikely to last for long and the rate of profit would tend to be uniform. An exceptionally high rate of profit in one place would lead carriers to increase their capacity, whereas an exceptionally low rate would lead to aeroplanes being transferred elsewhere. This does not happen to the degree or with the speed that it should because of the bilateral agreements that deny freedom of entry and the related pooling agreements and other commercial arrangements which often determine the level of capacity on a route.

Another reason why the international airlines react so weakly to economic incentives is that most of them are state-owned and nearly all of them have, as a result of regulation and protection, become pre-occupied with the maintenance and expansion of their services. Even when losses start to be incurred, capacity continues to be expanded and the airways notch up deficits year after year.

The failure to minimize costs, and to adjust capacity to

traffic, means that resources are not being allocated in the optimum manner. For example, if the fare is 25 per cent lower than the marginal cost (that is, the cost of producing an extra unit of output) on route A, but 25 per cent higher than the marginal cost on route B, it is possible by moving resources from A to B to obtain a net benefit which is 50 per cent higher than the cost of the resources that are transferred.

If, say, the marginal cost on route A is £100, the net benefit, both to society and to the airline, of carrying one fewer passenger is £25. This is the difference between the cost avoided (£100) and the fare (£75); and the latter represents not only what the airline would have been paid but also what the journey was worth to the (marginal) passenger. If the marginal costs on route B also happen to be £100, then the net benefit both to society and to the airline of carrying one more passenger is again £25, because this is the difference between the cost avoided (£100) and the fare (£125). Hence, if one fewer passenger is carried on route A and one more on route B, and £100 of resources are transferred, the total net benefit is £50, viz £25 on A and £25 on B.[12]

It may be thought that this has no bearing on international aviation because the general level of profitability has been low and, even in the most profitable regions and airlines, revenue has not been greatly in excess of (total) costs. Nevertheless, as long as some areas are more profitable than others it is possible to raise welfare by shifting resources in that direction. Moreover, there are many places within the industry where excess profits are being made. These are then used to meet losses elsewhere. The ensuing section shows that there are wide and persistent differences in profitability between different regions of the world and within regions among the various airlines.

PROFITABILITY BY AREA AND AIRLINE

Each year since 1975, ICAO has obtained cost and revenue data on the scheduled international operations of a substantial number of airlines. For instance, during 1981 it obtained comprehensive information from 75 carriers which together accounted for 76 per cent of the total seat-miles provided on scheduled international services. It then made profitability estimates for all the airlines operating in the seventeen groups of international routes that it distinguishes. The methods by which overheads are allocated between the groups are the same as those used by some carriers and, although ICAO's results are obviously subject to a margin of error, it is unlikely to be very large.[13]

There has been a persistent tendency for some route groups to be significantly more profitable than the industry as a whole and for others to be substantially less profitable. Between 1975 and 1982, the industry's revenue was 5 per cent less than its expenditure, including interest payments. But the revenue did not include the earnings of airlines from commissions and other miscellaneous sources which the ICAO does not generally allocate to route groups. When these are taken into account, revenue exceeded costs by about 2 per cent.

The most profitable routes appear to be those within Western Europe, although the figures are disputed by the Association of European Airlines (AEA). Here, profitability, as measured by revenue as a proportion of costs, was constantly above the general level for all routes. Earnings were, on average, 3 per cent higher than expenditure and incidental revenue appears to have been around the average level. Three other relatively profitable areas may be mentioned. First, there were the routes from Western Europe and the Middle East to Africa, where revenue was 2 per cent more than expenditure, financial performance was above average for seven years out of eight and equal to it in one year (1976); incidental earnings were high. Second, on the internal and connecting Asian and West Pacific services, revenue was only 1 per cent below costs, and profitability was at or above average in every year except one (1977); incidental revenue was significant. Finally, there were the local Central American and Caribbean services, where revenue exceeded costs by 3 per cent over the period 1978-82.[14]

At the other end of the financial spectrum were the routes between Canada, Mexico and the United States. Their profitability was relatively low for seven years out of the eight and, on average, revenue was 16 per cent less than expenditure. Other poor areas included the North Atlantic and the South Pacific. In both cases, revenue fell short of costs by about 12 per cent, there being only one year when the financial performance was as good as the world average. At long last, however, there has now been some improvement in profitability on the North Atlantic.

Within each of the route groups there are substantial differences in the relationship between costs and revenue for each airline. In the case of internal European services, earnings in 1982 exceeded operating expenditure by 10 per cent at the most profitable of ten airlines. At the least profitable there was a shortfall of 11 per cent and figures for earlier years show an equally wide range in results.[15] Nevertheless, Western Europe is a route group where there is relatively little difference in financial performance between carriers.

Huge contrasts emerge when the whole aviation industry is broken down not only by route group but also by airline, thus obtaining what may be described as airline 'sectors' (for example, British Airways' routes to Africa). In 1977 and 1978, the industry just about covered its costs, before allowing for incidental revenue. Only about one third of the airline sectors operated by the carriers for which the ICAO obtained comprehensive information had revenue which exceeded costs by no more than 10 per cent or fell short by no more than 10 per cent.[16] Moreover, during 1980 and 1981, when only about 90 per cent of expenditure was covered, 25 per cent of the sectors had earnings that exceeded costs by over 10 per cent or fell short by more than 30 per cent.[17] In other words, about a quarter of the sectors were outside a broad band of profitability which began about 20 per cent below the industry average and ended about 20 per cent above. Indeed, to judge from the figures for 1978 and 1981, about 10 per cent of sectors are at least 30 per cent less profitable than the whole industry or at least 45 per cent more profitable. This means that the best sectors are more than twice as profitable as the worst.

These figures do not disclose the full extent to which profitability varies within the airline industry. Each of IACO's route groups embraces a wide area and, in view of the contrasts that have already been discovered, it seems reasonable to suppose that there are significant differences in profitability within airline sectors. What is wanted is a further geographical breakdown disclosing the relationship between earnings and expenditure for separate airline routes. Unfortunately the only relevant information is scrappy and confined to the West European internal services. As might be expected, however, the variation in profits between routes appears to be very large.[18]

PROFITABILITY AND LENGTH OF HAUL

The variation in profitability from one part of the airline industry to another is not entirely haphazard and certain patterns emerge. One of these is that in Europe and probably in other parts of the world, longer-haul routes tend to be more profitable than those which are short hauls. The evidence for believing this to be the case is outlined in this section. It is taken from extensive sample inquiries by the AEA for the years 1975, 1979 and 1981. The last study (1981) covered 115 routes, which accounted for some 25 per cent of the traffic of AEA members in Western Europe. Except for the longest routes, there was a marked tendency for profitability to increase with the length of haul. When the results of the three surveys are averaged, revenue was 3 per cent lower than expenditure, including overheads and interest, on routes of between 125 and 250 miles. There was then an almost continuous improvement until, for routes of 870-1,000 miles, revenue exceeded costs by 20 per cent. Finally, on routes of over 1,120 miles, earnings were 6 per cent below costs.[19]

It may be objected that although short-haul routes appear to make a loss, they act as feeder services for longer routes and, therefore, help to improve their load factors and profitability. But in 1981, although not in 1975, nearly half of the routes of over 620 miles incurred losses and there was no very discernible tendency for the load factor to increase with distance.[20] Even the AEA does not really try to maintain that the profitable routes are supported by the unprofitable, but, when attacking the idea of greater competition, it argues that the reverse is true.[21]

There is no doubt that extensive cross-subsidization occurs within the international airline industry. Carriers earn abnormally high profits in some places, which are then used to meet some or all of the losses that they incur elsewhere. According to the study of airline costs and revenues which the ICAO made for 1982:

'In the case of European airlines, the revenue/cost ratio (including incidental revenues) for all international routes in 1982 was 1.04. In local Europe their revenue/cost ratio (including incidental revenues) was close to the average (at 1.05), while on their other major routes to Africa, to the Middle East, across the North Atlantic and to Asia-Pacific, the revenue/cost ratios of the European airlines (including incidental revenues) were 1.20, 1.15, 1.00 and 0.95 respectively. The differing revenue/cost ratios achieved by European airlines on different route groups appear to be determined by the competitive situation on each route group in 1982. On routes between Europe and Asia-Pacific the competition was such that neither the European nor Asia-Pacific airlines achieved profitability. On Europe-Middle East routes the European airlines could earn a profit because they were able to maintain a higher average revenue yield than the Middle East airlines. On the Europe-Africa route group, the European airlines were also profitable because they had much lower cost levels than the African Airlines.'

The same pattern was to be observed in previous years, except that the North Atlantic services of the West European airlines, instead of breaking even, made losses.[22]

Extensive cross-subsidization also takes place within Western Europe itself. The AEA's sample study for 1975 showed that eight out of thirteen carriers were operating both loss-making services and those where revenue was more than 8 per cent greater than costs.[23] More information, taken from a larger sample, would almost certainly have disclosed that cross-subsidization was more prevalent than these facts may seem to suggest.

PROFITABILITY BY TYPE OF FARE

On each route the relationship between costs and charges varies — and varies systematically — for each type of fare. Most airlines do not make any serious attempt to relate the different fares they charge to the costs that are involved in carrying the relevant type of traffic (this would, in any case, be a difficult exercise). Their aim is to charge what the market will bear. There is therefore a tendency for the standard, full-fares to be higher in relation to costs than discount fares. Because full-fare tickets are mainly used by business passengers, demand is not very sensitive to price and the airlines tend to keep fares at a high level. By contrast, the demand for discount tickets is highly sensitive to price because they are largely used for discretionary travel and it is here that the scheduled airlines face competition from the charter carriers. Hence the airlines try to keep fares low.

The only full investigation of this relationship that has been published was made by the CAA and British Airways. It covered six representative routes in Western Europe and was based on budget data for 1976-77. The methods that were used to allocate costs between different types of fare seem eminently reasonable. It is unnecessary, therefore, to discuss them here, with the exception of the allowance that was made for 'schedule convenience'. It was assumed that, but for the need of its first-class and other full-fare passengers for a frequent and convenient service, British Airways would be able to reduce its number of flights and consolidate traffic into large, low-cost aircraft. Estimates were made of what costs would have been if consolidation had taken place and also, alternatively, if frequency had been maintained, but British Airways had only carried full-fare traffic in small high-cost aircraft. The difference between costs with large and with small aircraft was the cost of schedule convenience and was ascribed to the full-fare passenger groups.[24]

As the existing frequency of service is presumably maintained in the interests of the full-fare passengers, it seems appropriate for them to bear the cost. But the case for allowing for schedule convenience rests on the assumption that full-fare passengers really do require services of the standards that are being provided. Such an assumption is questionable. On one of the routes, 53 return services per week were, at that time, being operated in summer and 46 in winter. Another qualification is that although wide-bodied jets appear in theory to have some cost advantage on dense, medium-haul routes, they have turned out to be not quite so cost-effective in the United States. This is discussed in Chapter 3.

The CAA study showed that full-fare traffic was fairly profitable on the three routes with the shortest hauls and highly profitable on those with the longest. Where hauls were shortest, revenue per passenger was 17 per cent greater than the cost per passenger, before allowing for schedule convenience; and it was 12 per cent higher after making this allowance. On the longest haul routes the figures were, respectively, 71 and 53 per cent.

By contrast, first-class traffic tended to be wildly unprofitable. On the five routes where there were first-class cabins, the revenue per passenger was 25 per cent less than the cost per passenger, even before allowing for schedule convenience, and there was only one route, which was exceptionally profitable, where revenue exceeded costs. Moreover, as the CAA study observes, 'the charter-competitive fares generally did not cover costs'.[25] These fares included part charter work for inclusive tour operators and individual inclusive tours through travel agents. The revenue per passenger for business of this type was, on average, 19 per cent less than the cost before allowing for schedule convenience and 8 per cent lower after taking it into account, but the shortfall would have been significantly greater were it not for the one route that was highly profitable. It is difficult to make any generalization about excursion traffic, which was the last major type, because, among other reasons, its profitability differed widely from one route to another. One point about the relationship between fares and costs which needs to be stressed is just how poor it appears to have been. On the six routes that were studied there were in all 28 different fares, but in only eight cases was the revenue per passenger between 85 and 115 per cent of the estimated cost per passenger (when no allowance was made for schedule convenience).

After the original inquiry was made, the CAA examined a large number of routes, not all of which were in Western Europe. The same pattern emerged: British Airways tended to over-charge its full-fare passengers and to make a loss on its charter-competitive fares.[26] It was discovered, for instance, that its West European Apex fares, which were introduced to ward off charter competition, did not cover their costs.

The work undertaken by the CAA has the obvious limitation that it only covers British Airways and gives no information on what happens elsewhere. Some information on the general position in Western Europe can, however, be extracted from a study of 117 European routes in 1979 by the AEA. There were eight routes that each carried more than 250,000 passengers per annum and which together accounted for approximately 30 per cent of the total passenger miles.[27] On these routes the full-fare traffic was by itself sufficiently dense to support an (average) service consisting of five aeroplanes per day in each direction when operated by B737s. This, in practice, would have been the minimum-cost service for the routes in question, as these were mainly short hauls. There does not therefore appear to have been any justification for a discount fare on the ground that this enabled carriers to provide a frequent service with large, low-cost aircraft. Or, to turn the argument around, there is no good reason to suppose that the need by full-fare passengers for a convenient service prevented the airlines from consolidating their traffic into big, low-cost aircraft.

The principal reason why it is more expensive to carry full-fare passengers than those travelling on discount tickets is the need to provide a greater number of spare seats. Those who buy full-fare tickets consist of business passengers and others who are prepared to pay a high fare in order to obtain a seat on the flight they select, even if they book at the last moment or, having booked in advance, decide to alter their travel arrangements. By contrast, those who travel on discount tickets are willing to commit themselves irrevocably and are less committed to use a particular flight. This means that it is possible to achieve a high load factor.

In the case of Apex traffic and inclusive-tour passengers, British Airways aims to achieve a load factor of 85 per cent on its scheduled services.[28] A certain number of seats are set aside for Apex and inclusive-tour passengers and this enables the issue of tickets to be controlled in order to prevent over-booking while leaving sufficient capacity for full-fare passengers. No such control, however, is exercised over the issue of excursion tickets which in 1979 were the principal form of discounting.

Even when a load factor of 85 per cent is used for all discount traffic (although this is almost certainly an over-estimate), it can be estimated from the study by the AEA that the revenue it produced was smaller than the costs incurred (assuming the same cost per seat mile for discount and for full-fare passengers). The revenue, however, from full-fare traffic exceeded residual expenditure by 25 per cent. It may tentatively be concluded that, on those European routes where traffic is most dense, the full fare is much higher in relation to costs than the discount fare.

Where traffic is more sparse it may be necessary, when examining the relationship between costs and fares, to assume that, in the absence of discount traffic, airlines would have to employ small, high-cost planes in order to provide the frequency of service that full-fare passengers require. This was the approach adopted by an ECAC task force. It tried to discover whether full fares were excessive by finding out for a number of European routes, belonging to five carriers, how they compared with the estimated cost of operating a service exclusively for business or full-fare traffic. A load factor of 55 per cent was taken as a representative average for this type of work and the frequency that the traffic would sustain was then calculated for each route, where necessary using any smaller aircraft which the airline possessed. When the reduction in frequency appeared to be too great, a judgment was made of the minimum acceptable level for the business market. Finally, on the basis of cost data provided by each airline, the break-even full fare was calculated and this was compared with the actual fare in 1979-80. On the six short-haul routes of up to 375 miles, the actual fares were generally lower than the break-even fares, whereas, on the sixteen medium-haul and long-haul routes, actual fares were, on average, 24 per cent higher.[29]

The relationship between fares and costs has been made to look better than it appears to be, not only because the figures for the short-haul and long-haul routes have been averaged but also because the figures for inward-bound and outward-bound journeys, which in many cases differ substantially, have also been averaged. When the routes are considered individually, and inward-bound and outward-bound journeys are treated separately, the published fare was over 25 per cent greater than the estimated required fare, or more than 20 per cent below it in almost half of the cases.

COMPARISONS OF REGIONAL COSTS

Not only is the relationship between fares and costs most imperfect in the international airline industry, but the level of cost varies greatly within the industry. This is only partly due to differences in the conditions under which carriers operate, as will be shown, and seems largely to be explained by the absence of any real pressure on the scheduled airlines to keep their costs to the minimum. The failure to control costs is certainly what would be expected in an airline system where competition is muted. Airlines can survive without being fully efficient; and they can even pay their staff excessive amounts.

The large difference in costs from one part of the industry to another is partly attributable to the large variation between regions in the price of goods and services which airlines purchase and partly to the wide diversity between route groups in their average lengths of haul. In its annual cost and revenue data ICAO allows for the effect which differences in fuel prices and landing charges have on the cost per passenger-mile in each of its seventeen route groups. It also removes the effect which differences in the mix of aircraft in a given fleet will have on direct costs and which stage-length and average speed have on both direct and indirect costs. Finally, variations in load factor are taken into account.[30] Even when these adjustments are made, there are still considerable differences in costs within the industry.

The figures for the international services which are operated by the airlines that belong to the seven geographical regions which the ICAO distinguishes should be the best guide to comparative costs. During the period 1978-82 the services within North America — the United States, Canada and Mexico — had the lowest costs. The regions with the next best performances were Central America, Asia and the Western Pacific and South America. Their costs were around 25 per cent higher than in North America. They were followed by Africa with costs over 40 per cent greater, Western Europe at 60 per cent more and the Middle East where (during 1978, 1979 and 1981) costs were around 70 per cent greater.[31]

When all route groups, including those between regions, are brought into the picture, a consistent pattern emerges.

Wherever North American airlines fly, costs tend to be relatively low and wherever West European, African and Middle Eastern carriers operate they tend to be high. Average adjusted costs were 7 per cent lower than the world mean for the five route groups where North American airlines fly. In comparison, costs were 5 per cent above the world average in the six route groups where West European airlines fly and, respectively, 14 and 26 per cent greater where African and Middle Eastern carriers operate, although the latter figures are each based on only two route groups. Costs were not very different from the world average where Central American and Caribbean airlines operate; and this was also the case where South American, Asian and Pacific airlines fly.

It therefore seems clear that there is a significant variation in costs between the operators from different regions, although the extent to which the West European, African and Middle Eastern operators have higher costs than those in North America is uncertain. The AEA has tried to justify the whole of the huge difference in costs between the internal services of West European airlines and the domestic services of the major carriers in the United States. It has pointed out that fuel is more expensive in Western Europe and that landing and *en route* charges are higher. Except for navigational charges, which are small, these factors were allowed for in the ICAO calculations. Moreover, the AEA figures show that, during 1980, the operating expenditure per capacity tonne-mile of West European carriers was about 75 per cent higher even when the fuel costs, landing charges and *en route* costs of the American airlines were adjusted to West European levels.[32]

Further adjustment is required because the average stage-length is higher in the United States, but even when the adjustment is made (by means of the CAB's regulatory fare formula) the costs of West European operators were still almost 50 per cent greater.[33] The AEA argues that the West European airlines have higher administrative costs because they are serving separate countries with different languages and legal systems. This does not explain why (unadjusted) maintenance costs per capacity tonne-mile were 119 per cent higher in Western Europe. It is also difficult to believe that the considerations which the AEA mentions wholly account for the fact that Western Europe's administrative overheads were 365 per cent greater and that its station, ground and passenger service costs were 315 per cent higher (although this must have been partly due to shorter passenger journeys within Western Europe).

The AEA also argues that:

'When the inter-continental operations of AEA airlines are compared with the international operations of American carriers, costs are close, emphasizing the fact that in a comparable environment costs — and fares — are at similar levels.'[34]

The AEA figures show that total operating costs per capacity tonne-mile were 19 per cent greater for the West European airlines than for the American operators. But the West European carriers have the advantage of a much greater stage-length and, when allowance is made for this, their costs were 32 per cent higher. The main reason for this disparity in costs was that the maintenance costs of West European airlines were 27 per cent greater, their expenditure on ticketing and sales was 52 per cent higher and their general administration costs were 112 per cent more than for American airlines.

It may be objected that these comparisons prove little or nothing because the general level of productivity is very high in the United States and Canada and it is therefore only to be expected that North American airlines will be more efficient and have lower costs. The reply to this is that North American airlines have to pay higher wages. International differences in productivity and pay should be reflected in the rates of exchange that were used by ICAO and the AEA in calculating their cost figures. Hence if American carriers have lower costs than West European, African and Middle Eastern operators, this should mean that the productivity differential is greater for airlines than for industry in general (or that the difference in pay is smaller). One problem with rates of exchange is that they fluctuate and this is why the IACO figures were taken, not for one, but for a five-year period. Although it seems clear that the West European, African and Middle Eastern airlines have high costs by American standards, this does not necessarily mean these standards are as good as they should be. That is to say, it does not follow that because the productivity differential between Europe and North America is greater in the aviation industry than in industry as a whole that the major American airlines are as efficient as the rest of American industry. This appears unlikely because, as will be discussed later, the regulation of the American airline industry appears to have had an adverse effect on productivity (and to have led to excessively high rates of pay).

Costs of Charter and Scheduled
Airlines

Thus far, the costs of scheduled airlines operating in different areas have been compared, but it is also possible to compare scheduled airlines with charter carriers from the same country. In their Cascade inquiry the CAA and British Airways made estimates of how much lower the latter's costs would have been, during 1975-76, if it had been providing a charter service. For instance, it was assumed that there would be no first-class cabin and that seating densities and standards of service would be at charter levels. It appeared that on the three routes studied the cost at which British Airways would be able to run a charter service was only about 10 per cent higher than the actual charter cost.[35] This, however, was scarcely surprising. In all the main areas where British Airways might display inefficiency (except perhaps for maintenance) it was assumed that the whole of the differential between its costs and those of charter operators (as represented by British Airways' charter subsidiary) was attributable to the fact that they were not providing the same type of service. Later KLM made a similar study for 1979. It claimed that when its costs were suitably adjusted they were only about 5 per cent higher than those of a Dutch charter firm which operated on the same route. But the figure was only as small as this because of KLM's lower capital charges. If this is disregarded, except to the extent to which it was due to cheaper aircraft, the gap widens to 10 per cent.[36]

An alternative approach is to try to find out by how much a charter operator's cost would be increased if it were to provide a scheduled service. One British charter carrier has made a study (known as Reverse Cascade) for a route very similar to one of those which British Airways and the CAA had previously investigated. The assumptions about load factors and the use of aircraft were either the same or very similar to the CAA's and the charter firm's estimates appear to be cautious. It even assumed a greater reduction in seating density, through the use of aircraft for scheduled work, than the original Cascade inquiry. The charter operator estimated that the cost per passenger for a scheduled service would be 120 per cent greater than the cost per passenger on a charter service, whereas the expenditure of British Airways was about 175 per cent more than the charter cost on its corresponding route. This implies that costs in British Airways were about 25 per cent greater than necessary.[37]

COMPARISONS OF PAY

The main reason that the scheduled airlines in Western Europe (and in Africa and the Middle East) have such high costs is that they employ their staff and equipment unproductively. It is difficult to see what alternative explanation there can be for the large difference in the level of administrative and maintenance costs of West European and American carriers. It is significant that whereas five leading American airlines obtained 8.33 hours of flying time per day from their narrow-bodied aircraft employed on domestic work, the figure for five top West European carriers was only 6.70 for their internal operations.[38] There is a subsidiary reason, however, why the West European airlines' costs are so high: the remuneration of their cockpit and cabin staff is excessive by American standards. In 1982 the pilots employed by the major American airlines received an average of $81,000. Lufthansa paid almost as much (around $77,000), Air France about the same amount ($80,000) and Swissair and KLM pilots received substantially more ($100,000).[39]

In order to make a valid comparison, however, it is necessary somehow to allow for the fact that the general level of earnings is higher in the United States. The best way of doing this appears to be to express, in percentage terms, the excess of the average pay of pilots over the average earnings of manual workers in manufacturing.[40] This is shown for the year 1982 for a number of airlines in Table 2.1.

TABLE 2.1

Comparison of Average Earnings of Airline Pilots and Manual Workers in Manufacturing for Airlines in Europe and the United States

	Excess of average earnings of airline pilots over average earnings of manual workers in manufacturing[a] *(1982)* *(per cent)*
United States (major airlines)	+ 370
Air France	+ 670
KLM	+ 590
Alitalia[b]	+ 590
Austrian Airlines	+ 540
Sabena	+ 440
Lufthansa	+ 420
Swissair	+ 410
SAS	+ 390

SOURCES: *Digest of Statistics*, International Civil Aviation Organization, Montreal; and *The 1982 Tax/Benefit Position of a Typical Worker in OECD Member Countries* (Paris: OECD Secretariat, 1983).

[a]Women workers are included in manufacturing earnings in the United States but are generally excluded in the European figures.

[b]Figures are for 1981.

The only airlines where pilots were relatively less well paid were Aer Lingus at 250 per cent, and British Airways, British

Caledonian and Finnair, which were all around 200 per cent. That pilots at these airlines received less in relation to manufacturing workers than in the United States does not necessarily mean that they were being underpaid. The CAB's Office of Economic Analysis argued that, because of the strong unionization which regulation made possible, American pilots' remuneration was excessive. As discussed below, pay cuts are now taking place and working hours are being increased; already working hours are far longer in the new airlines.[41]

There is also a tendency for cabin attendants of the West European airlines to be highly paid by American standards. The same method of comparison has been used as for Table 2.1 and the results are shown in Table 2.2. Once again the only airlines where pay was relatively low were British Airways, Aer Lingus, British Caledonian and Finnair.

Western Europe is not the only place in which pilots and cabin staff are very highly paid by American standards. This is also true of those international airlines from middle-income countries for which there are details. During 1982, pilots' earnings at Thai International were 43 per cent of the average for the major American airlines, but, during 1979, average monthly earnings in the manufacturing industry in Thailand were only 5.4 per cent of the level in the United States. This meant that, relative to manufacturing, the earnings of pilots were 700 per cent greater at Thai International than at the major American airlines. The corresponding figures were 380 per cent more at Egyptair, 360 per cent extra at Singapore International Airlines, 230 per cent more at Malaysian Air Services, 160 per cent higher at Aerolineas Argentina, 140 per cent greater for Varig (Brazil), 120 per cent more at Aeromexico, 110 per cent higher at Korean Air Lines and 60 per cent greater in Avianca (Chile).[42] For cabin attendants the figures ranged from 30 per cent more at Avianca to 410 per at Singapore International Airlines.

These comparisons could be misleading because, owing to a shortage of educated personnel, differentials are wider in developing countries than they are in the United States or other developed countries. But it seems unlikely that this is the full explanation. In many of the airlines from the middle-income countries pilots earn about as much as they do at British Airways, and in a few cases they earn more. During 1982, the average earnings of British Airways' pilots were about $36,000, whereas at Varig and Aeromexico pilots received well over $50,000, at

TABLE 2.2

Comparison of Average Earnings of Airline Cabin Staff and Manual Workers in Manufacturing for Airlines in Europe and the United States

	Excess of average earnings of cabin staff over average earnings of manual workers in manufacturing[a] (1982) (per cent)
United States (major airlines)	+ 44
Alitalia[b]	+ 246
Air France	+ 97
Lufthansa	+ 68
KLM	+ 67
SAS	+ 64
Sabena	+ 54
Austrian Airlines	+ 46
Swissair	+ 35
British Airways	+ 14
Aer Lingus	+ 12
Finnair	− 15
British Caledonian	− 13

SOURCES: *Digest of Statistics*, International Civil Aviation Organization, Montreal; *The 1982 Tax/Benefit Position of a Typical Worker in OECD Member Countries* (Paris: OECD Secretariat, 1983).

[a]Women workers are included in manufacturing earnings in the United States but are generally excluded in the European figures.

[b]Figures are for 1981.

Singapore International Airlines they obtained $39,000, and at Thai International, Malaysian Air Services and Korean Air Lines they received $33-35,000.

The very high earnings received by flying staff at most of the international airlines suggests that they have been able to increase their pay beyond the level that would prevail if competition between the carriers were more intense. The relative pay of ticketing and sales personnel also appears to be on the high side by American standards. At least among the West European operators, however, this tendency to high pay is less marked for 'ground' personnel than it is for pilots and cabin staff.

NOTES AND REFERENCES

1. *World Air Transport Statistics*, International Air Transport Association, Geneva, for 1977 (p. 8), for 1980 (p. 8) and for 1983 (p. 9); *Statistical Yearbook 1981*, United Nations, New York, p. 5; and *International Financial Statistics: Yearbook 1984*, International Monetary Fund, Washington.

2. With reference to this and the preceding paragraph, see the following: *A Review of the Economic Situation of Air Transport 1972-1982*, Circular 177-AT/67 (Montreal: International Civil Aviation Organization, 1982) pp. 3 and 10; *International Financial Statistics: Yearbook 1984, op. cit.*, pp. 103 and 123; *Labour Force Statistics 1970-81* (Paris: OECD Secretariat, 1983) pp. 22 and 23; and *OECD Economic Outlook*, OECD Secretariat, Paris, No. 37, 1985.

3. *A Review of the Economic Situation of Air Transport 1972-1982, op. cit.*; *Annual Report 1956*, British Transport Commission *Annual Report, 1956* (London, Her Majesty's Stationery Office, 1957) Vol. 2, p. 258; and *Transport Statistics Great Britain 1973-83* (London: Her Majesty's Stationery Office, 1984) pp. 19, 111 and 121.

4. *Report on Competition in Intra-European Air Services* (Paris: European Civil Aviation Conference, 1982) p. 95; and for subsequent text pp. 20, 21, 25, 26, 37, 41, 107, 108 and 113.

5. The Civil Aeronautics Board, the CAB, was disbanded in January 1985; the Department of Transportation and the Department of Justice in the United States now share the residual responsibility for its work.

6. Mahlon R. Straszheim, *The International Airline Industry* (Washington: Brookings Institution, 1969) pp. 26 and 172.

7. *European Air Fares: a Discussion Document* (London: Civil Aviation Authority, 1977) p. 61. The figure of 110 per cent excludes commissions and is not applicable.

8. This is explained more fully later in this chapter. The data has

been obtained from *Report on Intra-European Scheduled Air Fares* (Paris: European Civil Aviation Conference, 1981) p. 82.

9. Douglas A. Adkins, Martha J. Langelan and Joseph M. Trojanowski, *Is Competition Workable in North Atlantic Airline Markets?* (Washington: International Economics Analysis Group, Bureau of International Aviation, Civil Aeronautics Board, 1982) p. 6; and for subsequent text pp. 10, 11 and 13.

10. *World Air Transport Statistics, op. cit.*, for 1977 (p. 64) and for 1983 (p. 22).

11. *Survey of International Air Transport Fares and Rates, September 1982*, Circular 176-AT/66 (Montreal: International Civil Aviation Organization, 1982).

12. Because of indivisibilities the position is more complex than this suggests. The general principle, however, holds good.

13. *Regional Differences in Fares, Rates and Costs for International Air Transport 1981*, Circular 180-AT/69 (Montreal: International Civil Aviation Organization, 1983) p. 31; and *Report on Intra-European Scheduled Air Fares, op. cit.*, p. 94.

14. For 1975-82, see the following ICAO Circulars, which have the same or similar titles as in the previous footnote: No. 131-AT/39 (1975), p. 4; No. 140-AT/45 (1976), pp. 2 and 5; No. 144-AT/49 (1977), pp. 10, 11 and 15; No. 154-AT/56 (1978), pp. 10 and 11; No. 164-AT/61 (1979), pp. 8 and 11; No. 171-AT/64 (1980), pp. 9 and 11; No. 180-AT/69 (1981), pp. 9 and 11; and No. 188-AT/72 (1982), pp. 9 and 10. When the ICAO adopted a new method for allocating ticketing and sales expenditure there was an increase in Western Europe's costs and its profitability has accordingly been adjusted downwards during 1975-77. See Circular No. 164-AT/61, *op. cit.*, p. 14. According to the AEA figures revenue, including incidental earnings, was four and a half per cent greater than costs, excluding financial charges, over the period 1975-82. For this, see *Scheduled Passenger Air Fares in the EEC*, COM(81)398 final (Brussels: Commission of the European Community, 1981) p. 14; and *Civil Aviation Memorandum No. 2, Progress Towards the Development of a Community Air Transport Policy*, COM(84)72 final (Brussels: Commission of the European Community, 1984) p. 12. Interest charges appear to have represented about two and a half per cent of costs. See *Air Fares in Europe: Update of the 1979 Study*, AEA/517 (Brussels: Association of European Airlines, 1983) p. 2.

15. *Progress Towards the Development of a Community Air Transport Policy, op. cit.*, p. 12.

16. See the following ICAO Circulars Nos. 144-AT/49, *op. cit.*, pp.

10 and 14; and 154-AT/56, *op. cit.*, pp. 10 and 14.

17. ICAO Circulars Nos. 171-AT/64, *op. cit.*, pp. 9 and 13; and 180-AT/69, *op. cit.*, pp. 9 and 13.

18. *Air Fares in Europe* (Brussels: Association of European Airlines, 1977) p. 44; and *Air Fares in Europe: Update of the 1979 Study*, *op. cit.*, Appendix B.

19. *Air Fares in Europe: Update of the 1979 Study*, *op. cit.*, pp. 1 and 2; and *Air Fares in Europe*, *op. cit.*, p. 44.

20. *Air Fares in Europe*, *op. cit.*, pp. 44 and 46; and *Air Fares in Europe: Update of the 1979 Study*, *op. cit.*, p. 2, Appendix B.

21. *Facts and Figures April 1981* (Brussels: Association of European Airlines, 1981) p. 11.

22. ICAO Circulars No.s 154-AT/56, *op. cit.*, p. 13; 164-AT/61, *op. cit.*, p. 13; 171-AT/64, *op. cit.*, p. 12; 180-AT/69, *op. cit.*, p. 12; and 188-AT/72, *op. cit.*, p. 12.

23. *Air Fares in Europe*, *op. cit.*, p. 50.

24. *European Air Fares: a Discussion Document*, *op. cit.*, pp. 11 and 12 and Appendix 5.

25. *Ibid.*, pp. 11 and 12 and Appendix 5.

26. *Ibid.*, p. 13.

27. *Civil Aviation in Europe* (Brussels: Association of European Airlines, 1982) p. 55.

28. *European Air Fares: a Discussion Document*, *op. cit.*, p. 55.

29. *Report on Competition in Intra-European Air Services*, *op. cit.*, pp. 99 and 111-14.

30. ICAO Circular No. 180-AT/69, *op. cit.*, pp. 16-24.

31. ICAO Circulars Nos. 154-AT/56, *op. cit.*, p. 26; 164-AT/61, *op. cit.*, p. 25; 171-AT/64, *op. cit.*, p. 23; 180-AT/69, *op. cit.*, p. 23; and 188-AT/72, *op. cit.*, p. 23. Western Europe's costs may have been understated in 1978 because in 1979, when ICAO adopted an improved method for allocating ticketing and sales expenditure, there was a large increase in its adjusted costs.

32. *Civil Aviation in Europe*, *op. cit.*, p. 21.

33. *Ibid.*, and *A Comparison between European and United States Fares*, *op. cit.*, p. 7.

34. *Civil Aviation in Europe*, *op. cit.*, p. 22.

35. *European Air Fares: a Discussion Document*, *op. cit.*, p. 61.

36. *Report on Competition in Intra-European Air Services*, *op. cit.*, pp. 79-85.

37. *Scheduled Passenger Air Fares in the EEC* (Brussels: Commission of the European Communities, 1981) Annex 6.2.

38. *Civil Aviation in Europe*, *op. cit.*, p. 27.

39. *Digest of Statistics*, International Civil Aviation Organization, Montreal, No.s 288 and 297, Part D. It has been necessary to estimate the figure for pilots where other cockpit crew have been included.

40. *The 1982 Tax/Benefit Position of a Typical Worker in OECD Member Countries* (Paris: OECD Secretariat, 1983) pp. 28-49.

41. David R. Graham and Daniel P. Kaplan, *Competition and the Airlines: an Evaluation of Deregulation* (Washington: Office of Economic Analysis, Civil Aeronautics Board, 1982) pp. 123-124.

42. *Digest of Statistics*, ICAO, *op. cit.*, and Euromonitor, *International Marketing Data and Statistics*, London, Table 71.

Chapter 3

United States: the Triumph of De-regulation

A DECADE ago the opponents of liberalization of air traffic were able to argue that, although it might seem attractive in theory, it would not work in practice. This argument was illegitimate because it was circular and simply appealed to conservative instincts. What the advocates of regulation were saying was that liberalization should not be tried because it had not been tried. Even a decade ago this was not quite true. Although the aviation industry was for the most part tightly regulated in the United States, the tough controls that had been imposed by the federal authorities did not apply to services within the boundaries of the separate states. As their state governments did not follow the federal example, airlines were able to grow up in a largely unregulated environment within Texas, California and some other large states. These small-scale experiments in freedom had very favourable results. In particular, air fares were very low on intra-state routes. For this and other reasons the United States embarked on the wholesale liberalization of its air services. As a result, there is now extensive experience of what happens when aviation is de-regulated. The purpose of this chapter is to examine and evaluate this experience.

First, the way in which the industry's structure has changed under the impact of competition will be discussed; second, the level of fares and their relation to costs will be considered; consideration will then be given to the question of whether competition is leading to lower costs and higher efficiency; and, finally, an assessment of the effect of de-regulation on the airline industry's finances will be made — is de-regulation bankrupting the industry as its critics widely suppose? One question does not warrant extended examination, namely the effect of de-regulation on airline safety. Between 1978 and 1984 the number of deaths on scheduled services was only 55 per cent as large per million aircraft miles as it had been during 1973-77.[1]

Before looking at the effects of de-regulation it may be useful briefly to chart its course. Until the mid-1970s the airline industry in the United States was closely regulated. In order to fly on a particular route, an aircraft required a licence from the (former) regulatory authority, the CAB, which for some years had refused to grant any further licences. This moratorium came to an end during 1975 and from the spring of 1979 there has, in effect, been complete freedom of entry. Until the mid-1970s, air fares were also strictly regulated, but during 1976 the CAB took the first step towards de-control by abolishing all restrictions on charter operators save for the requirement that tickets must be purchased 30 days in advance. This meant that the scheduled airlines had to be given more freedom to introduce promotional fares and, during 1977, they were permitted to offer discount fares to passengers who could meet advance-purchase and minimum-stay requirements. By the spring of the following year, tickets of this type were available on virtually all trunk routes; off-peak and other discount fares were also being offered in some places.

Carriers were still unable to increase their full fares above the level set by the CAB's pricing formula, but in the summer of 1978 trunk airlines were permitted to increase them by up to 10 per cent above the level given by the old regulatory fare formula on those routes where there were four or more operators, and by up to 5 per cent where there were three or under. Finally, in May 1980, control over fares was effectively removed because the ceiling was fixed at more than 30 per cent above the fare formula. It can be seen, therefore, that de-regulation was not accomplished at a stroke and that it was already well underway before the Airline De-regulation Act, which was not passed until October 1978.

MARKET SHARES AND ENTRY

One of the principal arguments against de-regulation was that the largest carriers would increase their hold over the industry. So far, the reverse has happened although, as discussed below, the process may not continue. In 1978, ten trunk carriers accounted for 88 per cent of all domestic traffic, as measured by passenger miles.[2] By 1984 the share of the nine that continued to operate throughout the period had slumped to little more than 75 per cent and their traffic was only 5 per cent higher than that of the original ten in 1978. Meanwhile, the old local carriers entered longer-haul markets and increased their share from 8 to 12.5 per cent, the former intra-state operators have increased their share from 1.5 to 4 per cent by moving outside and two old charter operators, and the small commuter airlines which are no longer prevented from buying jets, have each grown from 0.5 to 1.5 per cent. In addition, about fifteen new jet airlines have started up. During 1984 they carried 4.5 per cent of all traffic.[3] Although their share is modest, it has expanded rapidly. The first of the new entrants (Midway) did not begin operating until the end of 1979 and People Express, which is the largest and most dynamic of them, has been engaged on a huge programme of expansion.

Before de-regulation, the local airlines tended to carry passengers over short distances into the major hubs of the airline network. Much of this traffic was then transported onwards by the trunk carriers. Since de-regulation, local airlines have established their own medium-distance or long-distance connecting services. It is sometimes supposed that, once this was possible, the local airlines would have a competitive advantage over the trunk carriers because it was they who carried the 'feed' traffic. However, the trunk carriers might themselves have entered local markets; instead they have withdrawn many of their short-haul services. Between the spring of 1978 and the spring of 1982 the (surviving) trunk carriers made a cut-back of approaching 40 per cent in their flights of under 500 miles.[4] One important reason why the trunk airlines found it difficult to compete on either short-haul or medium-haul routes was that they have had very few two-engine jets, whereas such aircraft accounted for the great bulk of the local airlines' capacity.[5] Jets with two engines have the advantage that, although they are small, their use does not involve any great cost penalty on routes of up to 800 miles. Hence they are able to provide a relatively frequent service in markets where traffic is not dense. Although the trunk airlines had too few small jets, they possessed too many wide-bodied aircraft, which can only achieve low costs per seat mile on long-haul routes. The excessive number of wide-bodied jets was probably explained by regulation. Competition had been confined to quality and service and, other things being equal, travellers prefered wide-bodied to narrow-bodied aircraft.

But the loss of market share of the trunk airlines is by no means completely explained by the composition of their fleets. It was also caused by their unnecessarily high costs and by the appearance of new airlines with low fares. Even where the same type of aircraft is flown, the trunk airlines tend to have considerably greater costs than the local airlines and to have much higher costs than the newly-certified airlines. In most cases, the entrants have set fares which are lower than those charged by the incumbent carriers. The latter have been forced to respond and, as a result, after allowing for the other factors that determine costs and fares, the average revenue per passenger mile, or yield, is 20 per cent lower on those routes where a newly-certified carrier has appeared.[6] Established operators, however, do not usually try completely to match the new entrants' fares, but content themselves with making selective reductions. One reason is that the newly-certified carriers have tended to provide a rather different type of service. They have mostly based themselves at secondary airports and many of them do not offer the same amenities as other airlines.[7] Nevertheless, because of their low fares, the new airlines, together with the old charter and intra-state carriers, succeeded in building up a market share of 10 per cent by 1984.

The fact that the newly-certified airlines and the locals have been entering existing markets suggests that there must have been an increase in the average number of operators per route and a reduction in the proportion of capacity in the hands of the leading carrier or carriers. This is the case. Between mid-1978 and mid-1983 the average number of operators rose from 1.4 to 1.8. The largest increase — from 2.2 to 2.9 — occurred on routes between the 22 largest hubs, which each enplane at least 1 per cent of total passenger traffic, but there has been a rise in markets of all types. Even between the smallest airports the average number of carriers per route increased from 1.1 to 1.5. These figures are confined to the number of carriers that provide a non-stop service, but, since de-regulation, carriers have been re-shaping their systems in order to provide convenient connecting services and have increasingly offered discounts in order to overcome passengers' reluctance to make intermediate stops. That the extra competition has been effective is shown by the decline in the proportion of passengers travelling non-stop between major airports and between large hubs and medium hubs. This has certainly not been due to any reduction in the quality of service: there has been an increase in the number of these markets that have a non-stop service and in the number of flights per route.[8]

Although there has on balance been an increase in the number of operators per route, this has been the result of substantial entry and exit. In mid-1978 the fifteen largest airlines then in existence had 5,832 routes. By mid-1983 they had ceased operating on 3,491 routes, or 60 per cent, but had meanwhile established 3,514 new routes (which means that the overall rise in the number of carriers per route must have been due to the expansion of small operators and entry by new carriers).[9] The period since de-regulation has obviously been exceptional, but the amount of entry and exit has nevertheless been impressive and provides further evidence that routes can readily be contested. This does not mean that the decision to operate a new route is a casual matter. Carriers generally expect new routes to make a good contribution to overheads within a very short time. Some require a fully profitable operation within six to eighteen months.[10]

HUB-AND-SPOKE NETWORKS

There is only one structural development that has taken place since de-regulation which provokes the question of whether the industry is moving in a competitive direction. Airlines have increasingly been basing their activities at one or two airports in order to construct effective hub-and-spoke systems where passengers, who have travelled on one spoke-like service, will be able to transfer at the hub airport to another 'radiating route'. As a result of this development, there has been some increase in the proportion of aircraft departures accounted for by the two largest carriers at those airports where one or more airlines have been centring their networks. For instance, between March 1978 and March 1982 there was a rise from 56 to 64 per cent at St Louis, because it is there that TWA and Ozark have chosen to locate their principal hubs. Over this period there was a significant increase in departure concentration at eight of the 22 largest airports, although in one place, where concentration appears to have risen (Chicago) there is a secondary airfield at which a new airline is located. At the same time, however, the proportion of departures by the two largest operators declined at ten of the top airports. Moreover, there were only six places where the two leading operators enjoyed a commanding position because they accounted for over half of all departures; and in only one of those places was there a single dominant operator.[11] This was US Air at Pittsburg.

That some of the top airports are dominated by one or two carriers is not as worrying as it may appear. Although airlines may be very strongly entrenched at particular airports, it does not necessarily follow that they enjoy any substantial degree of monopoly power. They may face competition (or fear competition) from airlines which do not serve the airport in question, but provide (or would be able to provide) a direct service between the places which the seemingly monopolistic airlines serve indirectly via their hubs. An example of this is Delta and Eastern Airlines which have a very strong grip on Atlanta. In 1982 they accounted for 80 per cent of all departures — the highest proportion for which two carriers were responsible at any of the top airports. But they now face substantial competition from Piedmont. It has not tried to break its way into Atlanta, but has introduced non-stop services between many of the places which Delta and Eastern serve by means of connecting services through Atlanta.

Instead of providing a direct service, the competing carrier may itself provide an indirect one via its own hub. For example, it may be possible to get from A to B not only on airline Y through hub C but also on airline Z via D. This strategy has also been pursued by Piedmont. It has built up its own hub at Charlotte, North Carolina, through which it provides services to the places that Eastern and Delta serve via Atlanta. Between the first part of 1978 and the first part of 1983 there was an increase of 480 per cent in Piedmont's flights from Charlotte and a rise of 146 per cent in the total amount of capacity out of Charlotte, as measured by the number of aircraft seats per week. The growth in capacity from Atlanta was only 20 per cent and, although this remains a far larger hub, the amount of capacity from Charlotte was, by the beginning of 1983, equivalent to 23 per cent of that out of Atlanta.[12]

MONOPOLY PRICING?

Although the developments that have been taking place in the American airline industry suggest, by and large, that it is competitive, the question remains whether the pressures have been strong enough to prevent monopoly pricing. If the American carriers had been engaged in general monopoly pricing, they would at least have tried to increase their fares in line with their average costs so as to avoid the losses they incurred. Between 1977 and the first three-quarters of 1983 revenue per passenger mile fell by 14 per cent, after allowing for general inflation. Meanwhile, formula fares, which reflected airline costs and showed approximately what would have happened to fares in the absence of de-regulation, remained about the same in real terms.[13] What happened, as the critics of de-regulation loudly complained, was that the airlines, under the pressure of competition, charged the marginal and not the average cost (see Chapter 4). Because fares were depressed, load factors were high, even though demand was lower than had been expected. This is discussed more fully later in the chapter.

The absence of general monopoly pricing does not necessarily mean that competitive pressures are uniformly strong. CAB staff have investigated the relationship between the yield and the extent to which the market is concentrated. Allowance was made, by means of regression analysis, for the other factors that might help to determine the level of concentration. They included the length of route, the volume of traffic, the presence of a newly certified carrier and valuation of time by travellers, as represented by household income in the cities being served. All of the factors turned out to have the expected relationship with the revenue per passenger mile and to be statistically significant. It was found, for instance, that the yield declined dramatically with distance and also fell as the volume of traffic increased.[14]

Because the size of the market and the number of competing airlines were so closely related, it was impossible to determine the separate effect which each of these factors had on the levels of fares. When concentration was taken to be independent of density, the yield appeared in comparison with monopoly markets to be 6 per cent lower where there were two competitors of equal size, which was approximately the average level of concentration in large markets. Moreover, it seemed to be 11 per cent smaller on routes with the equivalent of four firms of equal size, which was the maximum number where there were any substantial number of observations. When, alternatively, it was assumed that concentration was not independent of density, market concentration did not have a significant effect on the yield. In this case fares in a market with 25 passengers per day were 12 per cent higher than those in a market with 500 passengers per day. This compared with only a 6 per cent increase when density and concentration were taken to be independent. As big, low-cost aeroplanes are used in dense markets, an increase of 6 per cent seems suspiciously small. David Graham and Daniel Kaplan, of the CAB's Office of Economic Analysis, summed this up by saying that, although they had been unable to discover the precise influence of market concentration on fares, they had found the maximum possible effect:

'In the second quarter of 1981, fares in relatively unconcentrated markets were no more than 10 per cent lower than fares in concentrated markets; the difference may well have been smaller.'

It is not clear that what is relevant and important is the fare differential between markets with the smallest and the largest number of operators. So far, the general level of fares appears to have been set at a competitive level; that is, at marginal and not average cost. If so, the number of airlines in the typical market is presumably sufficient to ensure competitive price setting and, in order to discover the effect of high concentration, fares in monopoly markets should be compared with those in markets with the average degree of concentration. The even lower yield in markets that have an exceptionally large number of operators could be due to the presence of one or two new entrants which are temporarily charging particularly low fares in order to win traffic and establish themselves. In the CAB investigations, allowance was made for entry by newly-certified carriers, but not by other carriers. There is another possible reason why, other things being equal, yields are exceptionally low in relatively unconcentrated markets: passengers and travel agents may exhibit a preference for the carrier with the most flights.

Hence, in order to obtain traffic, operators with relatively few flights may have to charge low fares. The CAB's economists found that the smaller firms in a market tended to have the lowest yields. It seems reasonable to suppose that firms with a relatively small proportion of flights are to be found in the least concentrated markets and that their presence may depress the average yield.[15]

COSTS, FARES AND STANDARDS
OF SERVICE

The absence of any firm evidence that fares are exceptionally high in monopoly markets does not necessarily mean that yields reflect costs. Under regulation, the CAB deliberately adopted a price-setting formula which produced fares that were too high for long-haul markets and too low for routes below 400 miles. Moreover, the standard fare for each route depended solely on distance, although it is by no means the only factor which needs to be taken into consideration. Even when regulation was at its tightest, the yield in each market was not necessarily equal to the one that the CAB formula produced because, for instance, discount tickets were sometimes available. Nevertheless, the formula fares provide a yardstick which allows comparison with the average revenue per passenger mile obtained after de-regulation. Just because the yardstick is known to be biased and unsophisticated, it is possible to see whether the yield deviates in the direction that is economically appropriate.

During the year ending in mid-1983, the yield in smaller markets fell steadily from 12-14 per cent above the formula level for distances of below 400 miles to 25 per cent below for routes of over 1,500 miles. In medium-size markets, yields also declined steadily from 5 per cent below the formula figure in short-haul markets to 35 per cent below where hauls were long. In the biggest markets, the yield was 29 per cent below the formula fare in short-distance markets and 40 per cent lower for long-haul routes, but only 20 per cent under the formula level for medium-haul routes. This aberration was partly due to the large proportion of services to New York, Chicago and Washington, where aircraft landings were restricted and the incumbent operators were able to charge a premium of about 5 per cent.[16] Thus, except for one special case, yield had the appropriate relationship with the formula fare level: there was a decline in the yield as a proportion of the formula fare as the length of haul increased.

Within each range band the yield represented a steadily decreasing proportion of the formula figure as markets became larger. For example, where hauls were of medium length, it fell from 10 per cent above the formula figure in the smallest markets to 20 per cent below in the largest. This is a further reason for supposing that charges reflect costs, because the CAB formula made no allowance for the way in which the cost per passenger mile tends to decrease as the volume of traffic increases. As flights become more frequent, the benefit to passengers in terms of added convenience falls off. Hence airlines will tend, as markets become more dense, to use larger planes which have lower costs. They will also provide fewer spare seats, because the more frequent the service the smaller the inconvenience of not being able to fly on any particular flight. This pattern was observed in 1982-83. On medium-haul routes, for instance, the number of seats per aircraft increased from 114 in the smallest markets to 158 in the largest and the load factor rose from 54 to 60 per cent.

As this suggests, competition should promote economic efficiency by ensuring not only that prices are based on costs but also that the quality of service is tailored to the demand. That it does produce this effect is suggested by what happens in tourist markets. Tourists are more price-sensitive than other passengers and attach less weight to being able to fly at a particular time on a particular day. It is therefore to be expected that on tourist routes fewer but larger planes will be operated, load factors will be high and fares will be low. A comparison of tourist and non-tourist markets shows that these predictions were generally fulfilled for both dense and less dense, long-haul routes.[17] They also held good for less dense, shorter-haul markets, but not for those where traffic was heavy. Here aeroplanes were smaller and the load factor lower on the tourist routes. This was probably due to the excess supply of aircraft and the relative ease with which carriers can enter tourist markets. Consequently, they tended to enter vacation markets to increase the utilization of their aircraft.

Another possible prediction about the quality of service under competition is that load factors will tend to rise as the length of haul increases. This is because the cost of holding extra seats available rises with distance, but the willingness of passengers to pay a premium in order to fly on a convenient aeroplane is unlikely to rise. Indeed, travellers may plan further ahead and be more flexible when making longer trips. In each market size group, the load factor steadily increased as the length of haul rose. For instance, in dense markets it increased from 59 per cent on short-haul routes to 67 per cent on those where hauls were long.

It therefore appears that, in general, fares reflect costs and that costs vary according to the standards of service which travellers require. It is also evident from the various figures that have been quoted that there were only a few types of market where the average revenue per passenger mile was above the formula level, namely markets of up to 1,500 miles with 10-50 passengers per day and those under 400 miles in length where there were between 50 and 200 passengers daily. On these routes the average yield was 10-14 per cent above the formula figure. This does not, however, provide evidence of monopoly pricing because, as shown, the CAB formula did not allow for the impact of density on costs and because the CAB deliberately adopted a method which understated the break-even fare in markets of under 400 miles. As a result, the local service airlines were permitted to fix their fares 30 per cent above the formula level.

Although there is a general tendency for fares to reflect costs, this does not necessarily mean that the relationship is particularly close. To discover the extent to which fares reflect costs, it would be necessary to have direct information on revenue and expenditure of airlines for individual routes. This is not available. It should also be noted that what has been discussed is the average revenue per passenger mile, or yield; although this has sometimes been loosely referred to as the 'fare'. Because of the wide availability of discount tickets that are much less expensive than standard tickets, the standard fare per mile is generally substantially higher than the yield. It is therefore possible that, even if yields are for the most part reasonable, standard fares have been pushed up to an excessively high level. It has been suggested that this has happened and that the American airlines engage in price discrimination by overcharging those who buy standard tickets, because they are mainly business passengers and hence largely insensitive to the level of fares.

PRICE DISCRIMINATION

Some information on standard fares has been gathered by the CAA. The authority looked at all routes out of New York and Atlanta where there were at least five non-stop flights per week with jet aircraft. It was found that, during October 1982, the lowest normal fare was below the CAB's formula level on over one third of the New York routes, but more than 20 per cent greater on half of them. The routes where there was a low fare tended to have three or more operators and to have more than 350 departures each month, whereas those routes where there were only high fares mainly had one or two operators and fewer than 350 flights. The bulk of the low fares were provided by new airlines (People Express and New York Air) and Capital, which was a former charter company. In nearly all cases where there was a cheap fare, the general level for normal fares was substantially higher; and the established operators seem to have been trying to compete by offering low fares with restrictive conditions. On the routes out of Atlanta, the standard fares were around 40 per cent greater than the formula level, even disregarding those where hauls were very short. Fares were closely related to distance and other factors do not appear to have had any great influence.[18]

It seems evident that those who buy standard tickets usually pay considerably more than they would if regulation had continued, although where there are new airlines, as there are on a significant number of routes in and out of New York, they have the opportunity of obtaining very cheap travel. This opportunity has been growing as low-cost airlines have extended their operations. Moreover, it would be wrong to jump to the conclusion that because standard fares are mainly above the formula level this necessarily means that discrimination is taking place. It is legitimate that those passengers who require a frequent service, and want to be sure of obtaining a seat, should pay more if they put the airline to the expense of operating small high-cost aeroplanes and providing sufficient seats to accommodate late-comers. There only appear to have been a few routes out of New York where standard fares were generally very high in spite of a large volume of traffic, for instance to Chicago where, ignoring Capital, the standard fare was 44 per cent above the formula level. In the case of the Atlanta services, fares must have been very high even where traffic was dense.

It seems probable that in some places price discrimination is taking place. But it is important to remember (i) that only about 20 per cent of passengers now pay the full fare and (ii) that discrimination may be deterred by competition. Two of the new airlines that began by providing a 'no-frills' service — New York Air and Midway, which is based in Chicago — are now trying to up-grade their standards of service and capture business traffic.

PAY AND EFFICIENCY

Those who advocated de-regulation argued strongly that it would lead to higher efficiency and lower costs. This section examines whether their hopes have been realized.

The civil aviation industry has been characterized by rapid technical progress. The period before de-regulation witnessed substantial gains in output per unit of input — or substantial reductions in cost per unit of output — after allowing for the rise in the price of inputs. Nevertheless, there is reason to believe that the industry was not operating at maximum efficiency. The passenger load factor was low. Between 1967 and 1976 it averaged only 52.4 per cent partly because, since prices were tightly controlled, the carriers competed through quality of service.[19] The cost of providing capacity also appears to have been excessive. This is scarcely surprising. Because of regulation, low-cost airlines were prevented from entering new routes; and the system by which fares were adjusted, in line with the change in the industry's costs, meant that each operator needed to be only as efficient as the other protected carriers. In addition to a low level of efficiency it also appears that regulation enabled airline workers to obtain excessively large pay increases. Between 1957 and 1977, pay at the American trunk airlines increased about 45 per cent more than in manufacturing industry; and for the local carriers the figure was even higher. There is evidence that by the end of the period, airline employees were receiving substantially more than comparable workers elsewhere.[20]

During the first phase of de-regulation there was a spectacular rise in the proportion of seats filled. In 1976, the passenger load factor stood at 54.8 per cent and during 1977, when restrictions on discount fares were greatly eased, there was a slight increase to 55.8 per cent. By the beginning of 1978, discount fares aimed at filling up empty seats had become widely available and, during that year, the load factor shot up to 61.0 per cent. In 1979, it reached 62.8 per cent, although this was largely attributable to a strike at United Airlines and the temporary grounding of DC10s. There was, however, very little fall in real costs per capacity tonne-mile. Between 1977 and 1979 the trunk and local airlines achieved a cut of only 1 per cent.[21] This was a much slower rate of reduction than between 1972 and 1977 when unit costs fell by 8.5 per cent. It should be noted that over this period low-cost, wide-bodied jets were introduced on an extensive scale.

Nevertheless there is no reason to believe that at the outset de-regulation had a favourable effect on operating efficiency. This is scarcely surprising, for it was not until 1980 that the market share of the trunk airlines fell substantially, following the virtual abolition of entry restrictions in the previous year.

During the second phase of de-regulation there has been no further increase in the proportion of seats occupied but, on the contrary, some decline. In 1981, when demand was extremely depressed, the passenger load factor fell to 57.6 per cent. However this was nearly 10 percentage points higher than in 1971, when the industry was also suffering from excess capacity and had a load factor of 48.1 per cent. In 1982, when demand was again depressed, the passenger load factor on domestic services was 58.7 per cent. By 1984, when economic conditions were favourable, the load factor had recovered to 59.2 per cent which, although slightly lower than in 1978-79, was high by previous standards. What is even more important, a drastic improvement in operating efficiency seems to have begun; and the airlines are now trying to tackle the problem of excessive wage rates. Between 1979 and 1982 real unit costs were cut by 7 per cent and it seems likely that there was a substantial reduction in 1983 and 1984. During the twelve months ending in September 1984 the number of employees per million seat miles was 10 per cent lower than in 1982.[22]

The trunk carriers were galvanized into action by their loss of market share and by their dire financial problems. Moreover, they were set an example by the new low-cost carriers which have been entering their routes. Had it not been for de-regulation their markets would have been safe and they would have had no example to follow, apart from that of the intra-state operators. These charged very low fares, but this could always be explained away and attributed to special factors. It will be seen that de-regulation cannot be held responsible for the industry's financial problems, but the problems would doubtless have been less serious, and the

pressure for reduction of costs less intense, if regulation had
continued and fares had been increased in line with costs.

COMPARATIVE COSTS: NEW AND ESTABLISHED
AIRLINES

That the costs of the newly-certified carriers were lower than
those of the incumbent airlines is apparent from the CAB's
investigations. The CAB estimated that, during 1980-81, the
fully-allocated cost per *seat* for a 200 mile journey using a B737
was about 120 per cent higher at United, the biggest carrier,
than at Southwest, which is the largest of the old intra-state
operators. At Piedmont, which is a former local-service airline,
the cost per seat, again using a B737, was around 60 per cent
higher than for Southwest. It appeared from figures for all
operations that People Express and World Airways — an old
charter company — had costs per seat mile which, allowing
for the way in which these costs decline with distance, were
about as low as those of Southwest. Among the other
important new entrants, two had costs which, although higher
than Southwest's, were decidedly low (Muse and Capitol) and
two had costs that were similar to Piedmont's (PSA and Air
Florida). This left three concerns out of the total of ten which
did not appear to have particularly low costs and it is
interesting to observe that they included Midway and New
York Air which have now decided to upgrade their service
and compete for business traffic.[23]

One of the reasons why some of the entrants have such low
costs is that their standards of service tend to be lower than
those of the incumbents. They have higher seating densities
and do not provide hot meals or even, in some cases, free
snacks and drinks. Southwest and People Express do not pass
baggage over to connecting flights of other operators, or
provide through-booking facilities. Over half of the new
entrants based themselves at a secondary airport. To say,
however, that the new airlines tend to provide a lower standard
of service is to some extent misleading. It is a deliberate
strategy which serves to enhance, and not reduce, the welfare

of travellers. What People Express and Southwest have done is to adopt a policy of 'unbundling', by which is meant stripping out all amenities and facilities that are not absolutely essential and which are then either charged for separately, like the handling of baggage, or not provided at all, like hot meals. This means that those who want to travel at minimum cost are now able to do so and that those who have no need for a particular facility, or do not value it sufficiently highly to pay the price, do not have to help meet its cost. In this way the consumer's range of choice is extended and there is an improvement in welfare.

Moreover, standards of service are by no means the only reason why the costs of entrants are generally low. They tend to use their staff more efficiently. Southwest's pilots fly about 75 hours per month and at People Express and the other new carriers the figure is around 70 hours. By contrast, during 1981 United and the other trunk airlines paid their pilots for 75-80 hours, but only obtained around 45 hours of flying time. The figure was so low, and had declined from 60-65 in the early 1960s, because of strong unionization and work rules that had become increasingly restrictive.

The efficient use of ground staff was also inhibited by restrictive practices. According to the CAB's Office of Economic Analysis:

'A variety of work rules have been developed that narrowly define various jobs and consequently limit the ability of airlines to assign their employees efficiently. For example, in some cases, baggage handlers are prohibited from performing clean-up operations while employees that clean up the terminal area are prohibited from cleaning aircraft interiors. In other cases, airlines are required to employ licensed mechanics to assure that an aircraft has clearance when it is pulled away from the gate prior to departure. This inflexibility is compounded by restrictions on the extent to which airlines can employ part time employees.'[24]

By contrast, there are no unions or restrictive arrangements at the new-entrant airlines. People Express and Southwest have reduced their overhead costs to a very low level because, among other reasons, they are very tightly staffed and economically managed. There were no secretaries at People Express! The newly-established airlines have also had lower costs because their pilots have only been paid about 40 per cent of the general average. This was partly because seniority had not been accumulated, but even at Southwest, which has been established longer, pilots obtained no more than 70 per cent of the average wage at the major airlines.[25]

It was not until the autumn of 1981 that the trunk airlines and local airlines began to secure changes in restrictive work rules and manning arrangements. The process began at United which negotiated a new contract enabling it to make small increases in the flying time of their pilots and to operate its B737s, and the new B767s, with two-man crews. Hitherto three men had been employed, although the local airlines had only two pilots on their two-engine aircraft. After the productivity deal at United, progress with the re-negotiation of restrictive arrangements was slow owing to resistance from the unions. During 1983, however, there was a breakthrough because many carriers were in a weak financial position and had to reduce costs in order to survive. Continental, one of the smaller trunk airlines, was the most striking case. It filed for bankruptcy and then cut salaries in half and increased working hours. But what has happened at United and American Airlines, the two largest carriers, has been more typical. They have managed to secure agreement with both their union and non-union employees that newly-hired staff will be paid between 20 and 50 per cent less than existing staff. The only group of workers in the two companies which resisted was United's pilots, but even they were forced to concede, during 1985, after a lengthy strike. Both of the airlines have provided existing staff with financial inducements to leave. Other airlines where important concessions on pay and productivity have been reached include Eastern, Western, Pan Am, TWA and Frontier.[26]

FINANCIAL STORY

The final aspect of de-regulation considered here is the effect that it has had on the financial position of the airlines. This was none too healthy when regulation was in force. Between 1970 and 1975 the rate of return of the major American carriers was only 8.8 per cent as against 12.5 per cent for all non-financial corporations in the United States.[27] In spite of this, the airlines did not have any difficulty in financing their capital expenditure. They may have been viewed as a safe investment because of regulation and the way in which the CAB had come to the assistance of carriers that were in financial difficulties. Routes, for instance, were awarded to financially weak airlines in the hope that this would improve their position. Similarly, because of their protected position, the airlines were able to raise abnormally large amounts of money through loans and loan stock. The industry's debt-to-equity ratio consistently exceeded 50:50 while the ratio for manufacturing was only about 30:70. As the interest payments on the loans of the airlines were eroded by inflation the industry managed to pay sufficient dividends to satisfy investors, in spite of its meagre profits.[28]

During the first phase of de-regulation there was an improvement in the industry's profitability. Between 1976 and 1978, the operating surplus on domestic operations rose from $575 million to $1 billion, although when this is expressed as a proportion of turnover the improvement was only from 4.1 to 5.6 per cent.[29] This rise is often attributed to de-regulation which resulted in an improved load factor because of the sale of discount tickets. But, if anything, the discount fares appear to have reduced profitability because the fall in revenue per passenger mile was probably as large or larger than the consequent increase in the volume of traffic. If so, the discount fares served to depress the industry's net earnings because the extra traffic must have led to some increase in expenditure. That revenue was not increased, and may have been reduced below the level which would otherwise have been attained, seems likely because, after allowing for inflation, passenger receipts grew by 6.9 per cent in 1979, whereas there were rises of 11.9 per cent in 1976 and 7.5 per cent in 1977. During these years the growth in real disposable income was similar to that in 1978, but there was, by contrast, little or no decline in the real yield.[30] Furthermore, estimates of the sensitivity of demand to changes in fares since de-regulation shows that a price reduction by a given percentage leads to a less than proportionate increase in airline traffic.[31]

After 1978 the industry's profitability rapidly deteriorated. In 1979, the operating surplus on domestic operations was down to $130 million, in 1980 there was no profit whatsoever and in 1981 there was a loss of $265 million which, during 1982, peaked at $750 million. In 1983, the loss fell sharply to $175 million; and in 1984, profits must have been at a record level. During the twelve months that ended in September 1984 those major airlines that were largely engaged in domestic work had an operating surplus of $2 billion. This represented 6.9 per cent of their turnover as against 6.7 per cent in 1978.[32]

Just as it would be wrong to attribute the high profits in 1978 and 1984 to de-regulation, so it would be wrong to jump to the conclusion that it was to blame for the industry's poor financial results between 1979 and 1983. Three main contributory factors can be identified. First, the airlines suffered a heavy blow by the 100 per cent rise in the price of fuel between 1978 and 1981. In the absence of this rise, airline carriers' expenditure would, *ceteris paribus*, have been $4 billion smaller during 1981.

Second, the industry made losses because until 1983 the economy was depressed. Airline traffic is highly sensitive to changes in income. It appears that in the United States every 1 per cent increase in real personal disposable income leads to a rise of 1.4 per cent in the number of passenger miles flown. Clinton Oster and his colleagues looked at what might have happened if real personal disposable income had continued to increase after 1978 at its historic rate of 2.5 per cent per annum. In this case, traffic would have been 9 per cent greater during 1981 and, if the airlines had put on 20 per cent more capacity than required precisely to accommodate the extra passengers, the load factor would have been 59 per cent instead of 57.5 per cent. The industry's net revenue would then have been well over $1 billion greater.[33] Although it would be wrong to attach too much significance to this figure, there is little doubt that the recession played a major part in driving the airlines into deficit.

The third main reason for airline losses was that the trunk carriers possessed too few narrow-bodied jets and too many wide-bodied jets. As a result, price wars developed in long-haul markets, where the wide-bodied jets were employed and the trunk airlines had difficulty in competing with the old local carriers and the new entrants on short-haul routes. Even in 1982, when the industry was losing money most heavily, carriers with stage lengths of less than 500 miles earned an operating profit of $125 million, which was equivalent to nearly 2 per cent of their revenue. Medium-haul airlines with hauls of between 500 and 600 miles sustained an aggregate loss of $50 million, which was less than 1 per cent of their revenue. But the carriers with the longest hauls had a deficit of $640 million, which represented more than 5 per cent of their turnover.[34]

It therefore seems right to attribute the financial difficulties of the airlines after 1979 not to de-regulation but to these three elements. It is, of course, true in one sense that de-regulation was responsible for the industry's problems, because they would have been less acute if it had not taken place. If regulation had continued, fares would have moved in step with the industry's average costs, instead of dropping below as a result of the pressure of competition at a time of excess capacity. Higher fares would have led to somewhat higher revenue because an increase in fares does not result in a proportionate reduction in traffic. Although this is true it is also trivial. There are numerous industries besides the aviation industry where an increase in prices will lead to higher revenue. Nobody in their right mind has ever supposed that this inelastic demand automatically qualified an industry for regulation. Special circumstances would be required to propose this qualification and these circumstances are not evident in the financial history of the American airline industry. The industry's financial performance has certainly been poor during much of the period since de-regulation, but there were obvious reasons for this.

There were also good reasons why Braniff and Continental went bankrupt and, here again, it would be wrong to blame de-regulation. Most of the trunk carriers moved relatively cautiously after the Airline Deregulation Act had been passed. Braniff, however, believed that the amount of de-regulation would be limited and of brief duration. The Act enjoined the CAB to offer those routes which had previously been awarded, but were not being flown, on a first-come, first-served basis; and Braniff snapped up and began operating a large number of these routes. There was an increase of 50 per cent in the number of airports served during a period of nine months and massive investment in new aircraft both for the new routes at home and those which were also secured abroad. The rest of the industry thought that these moves were a big mistake. According to a contemporary article in *Fortune* magazine, the leading American business magazine:[35]

'Competitors predict that Braniff is going to bleed at the bottom line from an unhappy mix of low load factors, expensive introductory discount fares, and high start-up costs for training personnel and providing new ground facilities. Critics go on to note that Braniff has landed in some markets already overpopulated with carriers... As for overseas routes, Continental's Robert Six is quick to point out that Braniff is venturing abroad without the marketing muscle it carries in the US... Braniff executives from [Chairman] Lawrence down counter the sniping of their confrères with a self-confidence that borders on arrogance.'[36]

Thus regulation provided Braniff with the opportunity to make mistakes but cannot be regarded as the reason for its downfall. This was mismanagment aggravated by economic depression. (In 1984, Braniff was resurrected, but it has made large losses and already has had to retrench its operations. Its chances of survival do not appear to be very bright.)

Continental's bankruptcy was due to its failure to control its costs. Between 1978 and the twelve months before it went bankrupt in September 1983, its operating expenditure per capacity tonne-mile rose faster than any other major American airline.[37] When Continental went bankrupt it was, by some skillful manoeuvering, able to use this as a way of cutting pay and raising productivity. It has consequently transformed itself into a low-cost and highly competitive undertaking. During the twelve months after its bankruptcy it had a substantial operating surplus and by the end of 1985 its traffic was markedly higher than it had ever been.[38]

FINANCIAL POSITION

Except for Braniff, the American airline industry has weathered the difficult years between 1980 and 1983 and has emerged into the financial sunshine. But although the industry, taken as a whole, had a very satisfactory performance during 1984 many of the airlines that had entered since de-regulation were not very profitable or made losses. A few disappeared. Air Florida went bankrupt in 1984 and Capitol ceased trading in 1985. Muse has been taken over by Southwest, but now seems to be doing well. Moreover, most of the new airlines and former intra-state operators appear, from the figures for the period from January to September, to have had a satisfactory year in 1985. The only one of any importance to have an operating loss was Midway, and even here the figure was very small ($1 million) and much less than during the corresponding period of the previous year. It may therefore be the case that the new airlines have not only obtained a significant share of the industry's traffic but have become financially established. This is certainly true of some operators, such as Southwest and PSA, but others are not as strong as they appear. People Express, for instance, has borrowed heavily in order to build itself into the sixth largest American airline in terms of passenger miles. Moreover, towards the end of 1985 People acquired Frontier, which is unprofitable.[39] To begin with, a substantial number of People's routes were to places where, before its arrival, the airline service was not good and there was a large amount of road traffic, some of which could be diverted to air. During 1984, however, People Express entered a number of major markets where it is in direct conflict with the trunk carriers. It put on services to such major cities as Los Angeles, Chicago and Minneapolis. The major airlines responded by establishing fares that are 70 per cent lower than the standard level, but subject to tight restrictions.[40]

Most of the major airlines have become stronger and more competitive and some of them, instead of giving ground, are beginning to launch counter-attacks on the new airlines and the old local carriers. As noted, they have been increasing their efficiency and many of them have negotiated schemes for the reduction of pay. Their marketing has also become more sophisticated. Most of the big airlines have introduced frequent 'flyer programmes' by which passengers who travel long distances on their services obtain a free flight or some other concession. United and American Airlines have each enrolled 1-2 million passengers. The major airlines have also been eliminating the unrestricted discounts that crept in when they were under financial pressure and have established fare systems which discriminate more clearly between business passengers, who pay the full fare, and discretionary travellers who are carried at a low fare. The new fare scheme that was initiated in 1985 by American Airlines to counter the competition from People Express is the latest move in this direction. Competition is intensifying not only between the trunk airlines and the new entrants but also between the trunk carriers and the old regional carriers. American Airlines, for example, has started to put on services to smaller communities and is starting to move into Piedmont's geographical territory.[41]

It would be wrong to jump to the conclusion that de-regulation has failed, even if some of the new airlines or old carriers do not survive. It could be claimed that de-regulation has been a success because many of the trunk airlines have, under the pressure of competition, become more efficient and better able to defend themselves. It is possible, as has been asserted, that if those airlines that have been competing with the major carriers are forced to retreat and withdraw, the American airline system will ultimately become a cosy oligopoly. But there seems little danger that this will happen. Many of the airlines that have been providing competition for the old trunk carriers are, like Southwest and Piedmont, firmly established. Moreover, even if some of the new entrants disappear, other concerns are likely to take their place. Continental has transformed itself into an expanding low-cost undertaking and at the beginning of 1986 its parent company bought Eastern Airlines, which made it the largest airline group in the United States.

Finally, it is by no means clear that there is any longer a need for the new airlines to set an example and act as catalysts. The old trunk airlines may well be generating sufficient competition among themselves.

NOTES AND REFERENCES

1. *FAA Statistical Handbook of Aviation*, Federal Aviation Administration, Washington, Table 10.2 (1974); Tables 9.2 and 9.3 (1982) Table 9.7 (1984). Sabotage accidents were excluded.

2. After taking account of those that have merged the trunk carriers comprised American, Braniff, Continental, Delta, Eastern, Northwest, Pan American, TWA and United and Western; (Braniff finally collapsed in 1982). The local airlines comprised Frontier, Ozark, Piedmont, Republic and United States Air. Texas International, a former local airline, has been transferred to the trunk carriers in 1978 as it was subsequently absorbed by Continental. From the beginning of 1981 the CAB adopted a new system of classification in which the trunk carriers together with Republic and United States Air became known as 'majors'.

3. For these statistics, see *The Changing Airline Industry: a Status Report Through 1982* (Washington: General Accounting Office, 1983), Appendix 2; also see Graham and Kaplan, 'Airline Deregulation is Working', *Regulation*, Washington, May/June 1982, p. 28; *Report to Congress: Implementation of the Provisions of the Airline Deregulation Act of 1978* (Washington: Civil Aeronautics Board, 1984) p. 13; *Air Carrier Traffic Statistics* (Washington: Civil Aeronautics Board, 1979); *Airline Industry Traffic Statistics*, Merrill Lynch, New York, 1985; *Report*, Oppenheimer and Co., No. 85-162, February 4, 1984; and *Annual* Report, Regional Airline Assocation, 1982.

4. Graham and Kaplan, *Competition and the Airlines: an Evaluation of Deregulation*, *op. cit.* Northwest, where there was a strike in 1978, was omitted.

5. Elizabeth E. Bailey and John C. Panzar, 'The Contestability of Airline Markets During the Transition to Deregulation', *Law and Contemporary Problems*, Durham, North Carolina, Winter 1981.

6. See Graham and Kaplan, *Competition and the Airlines: an Evaluaton of Deregulation*, *op. cit.*, p. 204.

7. *Ibid.*, p. 126. Although it has been difficult for new airlines to obtain entry at a number of airports, the decision to use secondary fields has probably been deliberate. It is significant that People Express selected Newark's nearly abandoned North Terminal in preference to an ultra modern but more expensive new terminal. See Peter Nulty, 'A Champ of Cheap Airlines', *Fortune*, New York, 22 March 1982, pp. 130 and 134.

8. See Graham and Kaplan, 'Efficiency and Competition in the Airline Industry', *Bell Journal of Economics*, Hicksville, New York, Spring 1983, p. 121; and *Report to Congress: Implementation of the Provisions of the Airlines Deregulation Act of 1978*, *op. cit.* pp. 14, 30, 31, 35 and 36.

9. *Report to Congress: Implementation of the Provisions of the Airlines Deregulation Act of 1978*, *op. cit.*, p. 29.

10. *Deregulation of Air Transport: a Perspective on the Experience in the United States*, CAA Paper 84009 (London: Civil Aviation Authority, 1984) p. 13.

11. Graham and Kaplan, *Competition and the Airlines: an Evaluation of Deregulation*, *op. cit.*, Appendix I.

12. *Report to Congress: Implementation of the Provisions of the Airlines Deregulation Act of 1978*, *op. cit.*, p. 11 and Appendix A.

13. *Ibid.*, p. 123.

14. Graham and Kaplan, *Competition and the Airlines: an Evaluation*

of Deregulation, op. cit., pp. 199-203 and for subsequent text pp. 203-05 and 213.

15. In a separate study of 194 of the most heavily- travelled markets, where concentration was defined slightly differently, monopoly appeared to have a slightly greater impact on fares. Nevertheless, fares in monopoly markets were only about 7 per cent greater than those where concentration was at the average levels (Graham and Kaplan, *Efficiency and Competition in the Airline Industry, loc. cit.*, pp. 131 and 135).

16. *Report to Congress: Implementation of the Provisions of the Airlines Deregulation Act of 1978, op. cit.*, p. 24; and Graham and Kaplan, *Competition and the Airlines: an Evaluation of Deregulation, op. cit.*, pp. 87 and 204.

17. *Report to Congress, op. cit.*

18. *A Comparison between European and United States Fares, op. cit.*, pp. 8, 10-12 and 27.

19. *FAA Statistical Handbook of Aviation, op. cit.*, 1974, Table 6.18; and 1982, Table 6.6.

20. *Ibid.*, and Graham and Kaplan, *Competition and the Airlines: an Evaluation of Deregulation, op. cit.*, pp. 119, 120 and 122-24.

21. This information was obtained from the CAB.

22. *Ibid.*; and *Airline Industry Quarterly Financial Statistics*, New York, January and December 1984.

23. Graham and Kaplan, *Competition and the Airlines: an Evaluation of Deregulation, op. cit.*, pp. 104, 106 and 109, and for subsequent text pp. 126-27.

24. *Ibid.*, pp. 116, 117, 183-85 and 187; *Fortune*, 22 March 1982, p. 134; and 'Friendly Skies for Little Airlines', *Fortune*, 9 February 1981, p. 48.

25. 'Friendly Skies for Little Airlines', *op. cit.*, p. 48; Graham and Kaplan, *Competition and the Airlines: an Evaluation of Deregulation, op. cit.*, p. 109; and *Digest of Statistics*, International Civil Aviation Organization, *op. cit.*

26. Graham and Kaplan, *Competition and the Airlines: an Evaluation of Deregulation, op. cit.*, pp. 108, 182 and 183; *Air Transport World*, Stamford, Connecticut, December 1981, p. 59; *Report*, Oppenheimer and Co., New York, No. 83-597 (23 June 1983); No. 83-777 (12 August 1983); No. 84-72 (19 January 1984); No. 84-87 (23 January 1984); No. 84-630 (23 May 1984); No. 84-1104 (13 September 1984); No. 84-1235 (9 October 1984); *Financial Times*, London and Frankfurt, 20 March 1984; and *Aviation Daily*,

Washington, 2 February 1984, p. 178; *Economist*, London, 22 June 1985, p. 68.

27. Adkins *et al.*, *op. cit.*, pp. 15-18. The rate of return represents gross profits as a percentage of gross assets.

28. Graham and Kaplan, *Competition and the Airlines: an Evaluation of Deregulation*, *op. cit.*, p. 32; *Regulatory Reform: Report of the CAB Staff* (Washington: Civil Aeronautics Board, 1975) pp. 140-42; and Peter J. Forsyth, *US Airline Deregulation: an Interim Assessment*, Working Paper No. 29 (London: Institute for Fiscal Studies, 1981) p. 44.

29. *FAA Statistical Handbook of Aviation*, *op. cit.*, 1983, p. 124.

30. *Statistical Abstract of the United States 1982-83* (Washington: Bureau of the Census, United States Department of Commerce, 1982) Tables 690, 694 and 1098.

31. José A. Gomez-Ibanez, Clinton V. Oster and Don H. Pickerell, 'Airline Financial Performance Under Deregulation', mimeograph, p. 7.

32. *FAA Statistical Handbook of Aviation 1985*, *op. cit.*, pp. 131 and 132.

33. Gomez-Ibanez *et al.*, *op. cit.*, pp. 10 and 11 and Table 2; and for subsequent text pp. 7-9 and 25.

34. *Air Carrier Financial Statistics* (Washington: Civil Aeronautics Board, December 1982). Braniff was not included in the 500-600 mile group.

35. *Fortune* magazine is published in New York.

36. Alexander Stuart, 'Braniff's Dizzying Takeoff into Deregulated Skies', *Fortune*, 26 March 1979, pp. 52-54; and John R. Meyer and Clinton V. Oster (eds), *Airline Deregulation: the Early Experience* (Boston: Auburn House, 1981) p. 101.

37. *Report to Congress: Implementation of the Provisions of the Airlines Deregulation Act of 1978*, *op. cit.*, Appendix D.

38. *Airline Industry Quarterly Financial Statistics*, December 1984.

39. *Report*, Oppenheimer and Co., New York, No. 85-384 (12 March 1985); 85-2483 (5 December 1985).

40. *Ibid.*, No. 84-1104 (13 September 1984); No. 84-1312 (31 October 1984); No. 85-119 (24 January 1985); and No. 85-162 (4 February 1985); and *Stock Research: Airlines*, Salomon Brothers, New York, 1 May 1984.

41. Graham and Kaplan, *Competition and the Airlines: an Evaluation of Deregulation*, *op. cit.*, pp. 99 and 100; *Report*, Oppenheimer and Co., New York, No. 84-981 (10 August 1984); No. 84-1098 (11 September 1984); No. 84-1104 (13 September 1984); No. 85-119 (24 January 1985); and No. 85-123 (25 January 1985).

Chapter 4

Theoretical Arguments against Liberalization

IT IS widely held that the aviation industry has distinctive features that make competition undesirable or impracticable and which justify some form of regulation. In spite of the prevalence of this belief, it is remarkably difficult to find any clear or comprehensive justification. Those who take this view often seem to regard the proposition as self-evident and confine themselves to describing competition as merely wasteful or destructive.

Before setting out the arguments against liberalization it may be helpful to explain some of the economic terms that are employed. The *marginal cost* is the increase (or reduction) in total cost when the volume of output, however it be measured, is increased (or reduced) by one unit. The *incremental cost* is the increase in the total cost when there is a substantial change in the volume of output. The *average cost* (or *full cost*) for any level of output is the total cost divided by the total number of units produced, and the *average incremental cost* is the incremental cost divided by the incremental output. Costs may be either variable/avoidable, because they alter when the output changes, or they may be fixed in the short run because they are invariable/unavoidable, for example, advertising expenditure and capital charges on aircraft. As the time period lengthens fewer and fewer costs are fixed and more and more are variable/avoidable. In the long run all costs are variable/avoidable. The *short run marginal cost* is therefore the increase (or reduction) in total short run costs when output is increased (or reduced) by one unit and *short run average cost* is the total cost in the short run for whatever level of output is being produced, divided by that output. Correspondingly, the *long run marginal cost* is the increase (or reduction) in the total long run cost when output is increased (or reduced) by one unit and the *long run average cost* is the long run total cost for the level of output in question divided by that output.

It is possible to identify three broad reasons for not leaving the industry to the free (or not so free) play of market forces. First, it is often argued that, because the incremental costs of carrying extra traffic are very low, airlines will tend to reduce fares below their full costs and thus make large losses. Second, it is sometimes supposed that, because of economies of scale, the airline industry, or individual routes, will fall into the hands of a few concerns, which will then be able to exploit their monopoly power and charge what the market will bear. In the third place, it is held that, even in the absence of monopoly pricing, the number of flights will be inadequate on many routes and fares will be higher than is socially desirable.

These arguments do not sit easily with one another. On the one hand, it is argued that there will be too little competition and that the purpose of regulation is to protect travellers against exploitation by monopolistic airlines. On the other hand, it is asserted that competition may be too great and that the task of regulation is to protect airlines from competition which is destructive and disruptive. Advocates of regulation may say that to begin with competition will be excessive, but that in the end bankruptcy and heavy losses will lead to the withdrawal of most operators. This reconciliation of the seemingly contradictory arguments is unsatisfactory. Competition does not have a disruptive effect, after the initial adjustment has taken place, unless it is relatively easy for an airline to start operating on a route where it has not previously been flying. But if entry is easy monopoly pricing is unlikely to occur. It is therefore doubtful whether all of the arguments against unrestricted competition can hold good. Each of the three propositions will now be examined in turn.

MARGINAL COSTS AND PRICING
POLICIES

The most frequently voiced criticism of unrestricted competition among airlines is that it is destructive, because the additional expenditure involved in carrying an extra passenger — the marginal cost — is very low and hence there are continuous price wars. According to Melvin Brenner, a former Vice President of Trans World Airways (TWA):

> 'Even "good" load factors involve substantial availability of empty seats (for example, a 70 per cent load factor means that there are nearly half as many empty seats as occupied seats). Thus, a sizeable imbalance of supply versus demand is inherent in scheduled service, even at load factors normally regarded as "high". With the nearly-zero marginal cost of this ever-present inventory of empty seats, the pressure to price below full-cost is a normal free market response.'

Similar arguments have been put forward by the AEA.[1]

A diagram may be helpful here (see Figure 4.1). It is for an airline on a particular route. Fares and costs per journey are shown up the vertical axis and the total number of journeys and seats provided, during some given period, are shown along the horizontal axis. The marginal cost (MC) is very low until every seat is occupied at C. At this point it becomes vertical, which means that it is infinitely large. This is because passengers are not permitted to stand and in the short run no more aircraft can be provided. Average costs per journey (and per seat) are depicted by the curve AB. (It has the property that any rectangle bounded by the vertical axis and the horizontal MC line, and which touches the average cost curve, is the same size. The reason is that these rectangles indicate total fixed costs which will remain the same regardless of how many seats are filled.)

To begin with there are plenty of spare seats because the fare is F_1, which is equal to the average cost (J_1X), and only J_1 journeys are made. If the route were fully competitive, however, fares would not remain at this level, but would be cut to F_2, where they are equal to the MC. As a result the number of journeys would increase to J_2 but the airline would make a huge loss (F_2YZE).

FIGURE 4.1

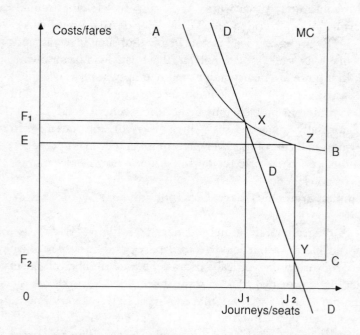

But why do airlines have so many empty seats? This is partly a consequence of regulation and of the absence of full-blooded competition. Although the airlines have over the years introduced discount fares with the object of filling spare seats and there has been a substantial increase in their load factor. The most important reason why the airlines continue to have empty seats, however, is that there is a pattern of demand which fluctuates from season to season, over the course of the week and from day to day. There is also some random variation in demand. Hence, if airlines are to meet the available demand at peak times, they will inevitably have spare seats and/or spare aeroplanes at other times. The appropriate response is for carriers to charge high fares during peak periods, which will tend to damp down traffic, and low fares at off-peak times, which will have a stimulating effect. Nevertheless, it would be foolish to imagine that there will never be any spare seats. There will have to be some to provide for chance variations in demand, and other seats will remain empty because, if the fare were always to be reduced to the level at which the aeroplane could be filled, it would sometimes not be worth putting on the flight, since its avoidable costs would not be covered. All airlines therefore plan their operations on the assumption that a substantial percentage of their seats will remain unfilled, although those that have introduced peak and off-peak fares, or other systems for smoothing traffic, budget for a lower proportion remaining unfilled. Because these empty seats are planned, and are in the main a necessary feature of their work, there is no reason to believe that airlines are going to bankrupt themselves by cutting their fares across the board in order to fill them.

If the airlines were to make a drastic reduction in fares, they would not be able to meet the increased demand and long queues and waiting lists would develop. Moreover, where off-peak fares, or some equivalent arrangement, had already been introduced the problem of excess demand would not be confined to peak periods. In these circumstances, it would be possible for any airline unilaterally to raise its fares and continue to fill its seats, because queuing and waiting are an inconvenience; passengers will be prepared to pay to avoid such inconvenience. It must be remembered that the cost of making an airline journey is not confined to the fare, but includes the value of the time the passenger has to spend on the aircraft and, what is relevant here, the time spent waiting for a flight.

If the reduction in fares were less drastic, there would not be general excess demand but, because of random fluctuations in demand, there would be frequent occasions when passengers were unable to obtain a seat on the flight they wanted. Hence it would almost certainly be possible for airlines to raise their fares to a level at which demand was choked off sufficiently for them to be able to provide those passengers who value their time highly with a seat on the flight of their choice. Even if there is strong competition between airlines, it will pay an airline to raise its fares so long as the reduction in revenue, through loss of passengers, is more than offset by the increase in receipts, through increased fares. As long as there is strong competition, passengers will be willing to pay a higher fare only if they enjoy a benefit which is at least commensurate with the cost. If it is not, they will desert to other airlines with lower fares and lower standards of seat availability. This means that the use of any given level of capacity will be optimal. Seats will only remain empty if the consequent increase in welfare — as measured by the extra amount that passengers pay — is greater than the benefit that potential travellers would derive from filling them, as reflected by the amount they would be prepared to pay.

Because some passengers value their time more highly than others, or find it easier to re-arrange their activities, it seems probable that no universal fare will emerge. What may well happen, as it has already, is that those who are prepared to book early and surrender the right to change their flight will be charged a low fare because, so long as airlines control their seat availability properly, this type of passenger will not contribute to random surges in traffic and involve the provision of reserve seats. If and when the places that are designated for these passengers have been booked, late-comers, unless they are prepared to pay a premium fare, will have to delay or expedite their time of departure. By contrast, those travellers who value their time and their convenience highly will want to be able to book, or change their booking, at the last moment and will be prepared to pay a premium fare. This will be necessary in order to compensate the airline for keeping a number of seats available for last-minute booking.

It may therefore be concluded that a substantial proportion of airline seats will inevitably remain empty and that if, after de-regulation, fares were to be drastically reduced, and the load factors were to rise to a very high level by present standards, some airlines would find it profitable to increase their fares. They would then be able to provide seats for those passengers who value their time and convenience highly and want to travel on a particular flight. It is a virtue of competition that the use of capacity will be optimal because passengers will receive the standard of service they demand and for which they are prepared to pay. This is not to deny that there may be problems of adjustment when full competition is introduced, but there is no reason to believe that just because the airlines have empty seats there will necessarily be indiscriminate price wars. Airlines will do their best to fill their spare seats, but not all empty seats are spare.

Excess Capacity

The opponents of liberalization must know all this. What, presumably, they are really trying to say is that airlines usually possess more empty seats than they require. It is certainly true that, if an excessive amount of capacity is provided, in a competitive environment fares will be driven down to a level where the amount which airlines earn over and above their variable costs is insufficient to cover all their fixed costs. For this very reason carriers will only buy, and fly, another aeroplane if the prospective additional revenue is sufficient to meet the extra cost that will be incurred, including capital charges on the aircraft. Hence, so long as their estimates of demand are correct, airlines will be able to meet their full costs because, even under perfect competition, the amount of capacity will be restricted to the point at which fares are sufficiently high for all costs to be covered. It is also important to recognize that, except in the very short run, when the number of flights cannot be changed, the bulk of the costs of the airlines are variable and not fixed. By operating fewer flights, airlines can quickly avoid the cost of fuel and landing fees and curtail their expenditure on maintenance. Over a somewhat longer term, employment can be slimmed down and aircraft can be sold or leased in a nearly-perfect world market, although they may not be worth very much if the industry is everywhere depressed.

The argument here may be illustrated by means of the Figure 4.1. The airlines provide a capacity of OC. Despite this, the fare is not reduced to *their* marginal cost (OF_2) because, even under perfect competition, it pays the airlines to maintain their fares at OF_1, where the beneficial effect on their individual revenues of a small increase in fares is just offset by the consequent loss of traffic. At this level of fares journeys will be restricted to J_1 and the number of empty seats will be J_1C. This may look like non-competitive pricing, but OF_1 will not be the fare at which collective profit of the airlines is maximized and, if allowance is made for the value which passengers place on their time and convenience, the marginal cost curve will pass through X. When the airlines provide just the right amount of capacity, and are in long run equilibrium, their fares will be equal to their average costs, as they are at X in the diagram. This means, of course, that they will be able to cover their expenditure in full and earn a normal profit. If, however, demand is weaker, that is the demand curve is further to the left, the airlines will fail to meet their full costs and have an incentive to reduce capacity. On the other hand, if demand is stronger and the demand curve is to the right, airlines will have an incentive to increase their capacity because they will be earning super-normal profits.

Although carriers will obviously aim to cover their direct costs when planning their capacity, they could disregard their indirect costs. Airline managers sometimes argue that this tends to happen. The problem of having to recover indirect costs is not unique, however, to aviation where they do not even seem to constitute a particularly heavy burden. Station expenses, ticketing, publicity and other general overheads account for only 25 per cent of total expenditure of international airlines.[2] All fixed costs of this type are variable in the long run and airlines will, like concerns in other industries, restrict their capacity and their expenditure to the point at which their revenue will be sufficient to meet their outlay. If they do not, those which have the greatest amount of surplus capacity will go bankrupt and those that survive will learn to be more prudent.

It may be argued that the problem is not the failure of airlines to take account of their indirect costs, but their tendency to over-estimate demand. It is difficult to see why it should be particularly hard to forecast demand in aviation or why predictions should usually be on the high side. But unless such a forecasting bias exists, it is to be expected that under competition there will sometimes be excess capacity, in which case a normal rate of profit would not be earned; at other times capacity would be inadequate and abnormally high profits would be made.

Should over-capacity occur there are powerful arguments in favour of fares being reduced in order that the spare capacity may be filled. It is clearly a waste of resources for aircraft to fly with more empty seats than are needed in order to provide travellers with the standards of service they require. Moreover, airlines will have little or no incentive to make realistic forecasts of demand if they know that, instead of having to bear the consequences of excess capacity in the form of losses, they will be able to make consumers meet the cost by increasing fares. Thus a system of fare-fixing which enables airlines to practice average-cost pricing and break even, is likely to lead to over-investment. This is probably one reason why excess capacity has tended to occur under regulation.

A NATURAL MONOPOLY?

An industry is a natural monopoly if its output can be produced more cheaply by one firm than by two or more. Civil aviation would be a natural monopoly if, because of continuing economies of scale, the largest and lowest-cost operator would ultimately be able to drive out all the others.

It is necessary here to draw a distinction between economies of scale on a particular route and those which may arise when an airline operates on a number of routes.

Few people, if any, have ever supposed that the most efficient company structure in the aviation industry would be for one massive airline to have a monopoly on every route. Even if this were the case, it would not provide a justification for the type of regulation which exists on international routes, since this affords protection to national airlines. Those who believe that there are important economies of scale in aviation maintain that the industry would, if competition were unrestricted, gravitate to oligopoly. This form of industrial structure is not, as experience elsewhere shows, incompatible with vigorous competition. But is it true that large airlines have a significant advantage over small carriers? At first sight it appears that they do. Among both international airlines and American domestic operators, there is a tendency for large airlines to have lower costs per tonne-mile or per seat-mile than small carriers. This, however, is misleading. There is also a tendency for the larger airlines to make longer flights and long hauls are accompanied by low costs. When allowance is made for this and other factors which affect costs, it does not appear that there are any significant economies of scale.[3]

Appearance can be deceptive: it is not so much the absolute size of an airline that affects its competitive position but whether its network is well structured. When passengers make journeys where it is necessary to transfer from one flight to another, they will tend to stay with the same airline. The connecting flight is more likely to be conveniently timed. There is felt to be less risk of baggage going astray and where, as frequently happens in the United States, each airline posseses its own terminal building, passengers do not have to travel from one building to another. Thus airlines with well-devised networks, will be able to feed traffic along one spoke-like route into their hub airports and then out along other spokes. In the United States the load factor tends to be slightly greater on flights where a relatively high proportion of passengers have transferred from, or will be transferring to, an airline's other services than on those flights where the amount of transfer traffic is relatively low.[4] Moreover, insofar as there are economies of scale at the route, as opposed to the system level (a topic to be considered below), an increase in the density of traffic will confer an advantage on an airline which carries a large volume of transfer traffic.

These benefits, however, will be offset, at least in part, by the adverse effect which a hub-and-spoke pattern of operations is likely to have on the utilization of aircraft. The provision of services that connect with, and therefore have to wait for, each other will obviously tend to depress the amount of time that aircraft spend in the air, as will the use of busy hub airports where there will be delays through congestion. In the United States, Southwest, which concentrates not on providing good connections but on short turn-around times, operates its aircraft for an average of eleven and a half hours per day whereas those airlines with hub-and-spoke systems only obtain between eight and a half and ten hours of flying time a day.[5] Furthermore, if the traffic between two places on the periphery of the spoke system becomes sufficiently great, it will become economic for a small concern to introduce a direct flight. It is therefore highly unlikely that the advantages of having a large and well-planned system are overwhelming.

BARRIERS TO ROUTE ENTRY

On the other hand, it seems evident that some economies of scale do exist on individual routes. So long as the comparison is confined to aircraft that are suitable for a given length of haul, there is a general tendency for the direct costs per seat flown to decline as the size of aircraft increases. This tendency is strong up to the point where it becomes possible to use a Boeing 737-200. Thus, over a distance of 500 miles, the average cost per seat is about 30 per cent lower for a B737-200, containing 130 seats, than for a CV580 which has a maximum of 56. Beyond 130 seats, however, there is little tendency for costs to fall further on hauls of up to 800 miles.

The B727-200, with 164 seats, is about as expensive as the B737-200 and even the 380-seat DC10-10 only leads to a reduction in costs of 4-13 per cent on journeys ranging from 400 to 800 miles. On hauls of 1,000 miles or more, wide-bodied jets lead to significant savings in costs. For very long journeys they are, indeed, the only up-to-date subsonic aircraft that are available.[6]

Even when airlines have a choice of aircraft and there are significant economies of scale, it does not follow that the most efficient arrangement is to have a monopoly operator using a giant plane. On some routes the volume of traffic will be so great as to warrant the use of at least two aircraft of the maximum size. On other routes the demand will be so small that the only way in which even a single large aeroplane could be filled would be to consolidate traffic by providing an infrequent service. Even then it might not be possible to use a big aircraft because the demand might fall. If small aircraft are used on secondary routes, there will be more flights and the service is likely to become more convenient. Travellers may therefore be prepared to pay a large enough premium to cover the extra cost that will result from using a small aircraft. In fact, the additional cost may not be very great if the provision of a high-quality service leads to such an increase in demand (at a given fare) that it is possible to have medium-size instead of small aircraft. Hence there is no obvious reason why large aircraft will carry the day. If they do not, and two or more small aircraft are employed, there will, other things being equal, be scope for two or more operators.

Other things, however, may not be entirely equal because, among other reasons, station costs per passenger probably decline initially as the volume of traffic rises. Hence monopoly carriers almost certainly have some advantage on routes where traffic is sparse. Nevertheless, even in those international (and American) markets where traffic is dense, there is seldom room for more than a few airlines unless, of course, they use aircraft that are very small and uneconomic. When it is considered route by route, the airline industry is incurably oligopolistic. But even if it were a natural monopoly, as it is on some of the less dense routes, this would not necessarily mean that the sole carrier would be able to charge a monopoly price. Whether it can depends on how easy it is for a new operator to put on a service. In the aviation industry this is not difficult, even for a new operator, because the cost of buying aircraft and spares is by no means prohibitive if secondhand aircraft are purchased. This is the way in which new private airlines usually establish themselves. When People Express began life in 1981 it acquired three Boeing 737s from Lufthansa for $3.7 million each, whereas new ones would have cost as much as $17 million.[7]

The only disadvantage of any real importance faced by an operator that tries to enter an existing route is that, if it begins by putting on a small number of flights, it is likely, other things being equal, to obtain an even smaller proportion of the traffic. This is because, in order to reduce search time, passengers and travel agents tend to contact the airlines which they believe offer the most flights. A study of 175 top markets in the United States suggested that, after allowing for other factors, a carrier with 50 per cent of flights between destinations has a 7 per cent higher revenue per passenger mile than one with 25 per cent and that the leading airline also has a somewhat greater load factor. Carriers may nevertheless be willing to enter and continue operating on routes where they only account for a minority of flights, because of the extra traffic that will be fed onto their other routes and the consequent improvement in load factors elsewhere.[8]

It is conceivable that entry may be more difficult than it appears because the established operators will resort to 'predatory' pricing. What they might do, when a new airline comes on the scene, is to reduce their prices drastically and then put them back up to their previous monopoly level once the intruder had been forced off the route. Such a strategy is only worthwhile if the losses during the price war can subsequently be recovered.

This may not be easy. Another interloper may begin operating or the original one may return and base its marketing on what happened to fares when it was previously forced to withdraw. Predatory pricing will only be financially attractive if the incumbent carriers can succeed in convincing would-be entrants that they have no chance of success. They will then give up trying and incumbents will be able to recoup their losses. Those who are practising monopoly pricing, however, may find that they are challenged at too many points at once or that their rivals adopt tactics which make predatory pricing very expensive. Instead of mounting a direct challenge, the intruder may appeal to a somewhat different market by, for instance, providing a low-price, no-frills service or by using a different airport. Alternatively, the new competition may take the form of a direct flight between places which the high-price carrier only serves by means of connecting services; or an airline, which already provides an indirect service between two towns, may begin competing more vigorously with an operator that makes direct flights, but is over-charging. The airline could introduce large, low-cost aircraft and reduce its fares for those making a through journey. There are so many possibilities that it seems unlikely that predatory pricing would prove to be an effective strategy.

Too Few Flights: the Argument

The final major argument against a policy of *laissez-faire* towards the aviation industry is that, even in the absence of monopoly pricing, the industry will provide too few flights and/or carry too few passengers. Output will be sub-optimal if the incremental cost of carrying more passengers, or providing more flights, is less than the additional benefit that is obtained. There are two main reasons why the industry's output may not be pushed to the point where the additional benefit is just equal to the extra cost. The first relates to the frequency of flights.

If, on any given route, flights become more frequent and convenient, there will be an increase in demand at the prevailing level of fares. So long as the growth in traffic is sufficient to fill the extra capacity there is no problem. At some point, however, the introduction of an extra flight will fail to generate enough traffic to fill the additional seats and, assuming that the fare is equal to the average cost per seat, the airline (or airlines) will begin to lose money. One possible response would be to use smaller aircraft, but, for the time being, it will be assumed that there are none available or that their unit costs are prohibitive. Another conceivable avenue of escape would then be to raise the level of fares. There is always a possibility, however, that the increase in fares will lead to a more than proportionate reduction in traffic and hence serve to depress revenue. While the fall in traffic will lead to some saving in expenditure, the saving will be restricted to those costs, such as meals, which are related to the numbers of passengers rather than to the operation of flights. Hence the airline may end up incurring larger losses than it would if fares had not been increased. Moreover, even if the airline is able to cover its costs by raising fares, this is undesirable because it will lead to even more spare seats. Fares should be reduced in order to fill the extra capacity that is being provided so long as the necessary fare is at least sufficient to cover the avoidable cost per passenger.[9]

Although the airline may not be able to make a normal profit — or, if it can, should not — it may well be desirable to put on more flights. Unless they are already numerous, and the services highly convenient, the provision of more flights will be of benefit to existing users. There will be a reduction in their inconvenience time, as measured by the interval between each passenger's ideal time of departure and his actual time of departure on the best aeroplane that is available. Hence it is reasonable to suppose that most of the existing passengers will be prepared to pay more. At first sight, it may appear that passengers are only prepared to pay what they are charged, but this is not the case: it is only the marginal users who are willing to contribute no more than they are asked. The fact that those who already use the service receive a benefit, which is equivalent to their increased preparedness to pay, should in principle be taken into account when it is being decided whether it is worthwhile to increase the number of flights. It will be desirable to put on an extra flight if the incremental cost is less than the additional amount that existing passengers are prepared to pay plus the sum which new passengers are willing to contribute. The size of this contribution partly depends on how many passengers there are and this, in turn, will partly depend on what fare is charged. The fare should be equal to the avoidable cost per passenger, given that the extra flight is being operated, or at such higher level as will restrict the number of passengers to the number of spare seats available.[10]

As a general rule it is undesirable for firms to provide goods or services if the amount that consumers pay is not sufficient, once they have had time to adjust their capacity, to meet their full costs of production. This is because resources will not be used with the maximum efficiency unless in the long run the price (the value which consumers place on the marginal unit of output) is equal to the long-run marginal cost, which is the value of the resources required to provide the marginal unit of output, including overheads, depreciation and normal profits. The long-run marginal cost must include overheads and capital charges because all costs are variable in the long run. Because the long-run marginal cost is comprehensive, any undertaking which pushes its production to the point where price equals long-run marginal cost will in the long run be able to cover all its costs and earn a normal profit.

There is one general proviso, namely that there are no continuing economies (or dis-economies) of scale and that the long-run marginal cost is therefore equal to the long-run average cost. If there are no economies of scale, or they have already bottomed out, the long-run average cost will be constant and equal to the long-run marginal cost. As it is being assumed for the present that there is only one type of aeroplane suitable for any given route, the main reason for economies of scale in aviation has been ruled out. Hence the long-run marginal cost and the long-run average cost should be approximately the same. Thus if an airline increases the number of flights to the point where the fare that it is able to charge is more or less equal to the long-run marginal cost, it will be able to meet its long-run average costs and earn a normal profit.

The distinctive feature of the airline industry (and of other forms of public transport) is that while the fare indicates the value which marginal users receive it does not show the full marginal value that is obtained. This is because, as noted previously, existing passengers also receive a benefit when an extra flight is provided. In most industries, existing users receive no corresponding advantage when output is expanded unless there is a change in price. It is therefore undesirable to increase production beyond the point at which the price is equal to the long-run marginal cost (on the assumption that this is equal to long-run average cost) because losses would then be incurred.[11] This is the reason for believing that, even in the absence of monopoly pricing, the number of flights will be sub-optimal.

TOO FEW FLIGHTS: THE REPLY

If the argument, even in the absence of monopoly pricing, that the aviation industry will provide too few flights is held to have force, the most appropriate response is not to regulate the airline industry, but to provide carriers with subsidies so that they can put on extra flights which, although they would involve losses, are economically desirable. There would then be no case for protecting from competition those airlines that received subsidies. If, however, governments are unwilling to provide financial support, protection could conceivably have some merit. Carriers would then be able to raise their fares above average (and marginal) cost on those routes where traffic is dense, flights are frequent and the welfare losses from withdrawing marginal flights are small. The monopoly profits thus obtained would, it is hoped, be used to cross-subsidize the provision of extra flights on those routes where traffic is sparse, flights are infrequent and where existing passengers would receive large benefits as the service was improved.

There is no reason to suppose that this is what happens at present. When the AEA route studies for 1979 and 1981 are taken together (or separately) there is no very marked tendency for the high-density routes to be more profitable than those where the density of traffic is lower. It is true that the ones where traffic was greatest were relatively profitable. Here revenue exceeded expenditure by an average of 10 per cent. But the figure was about the same where the traffic per route was of only average density; and in those where the traffic was second and third highest — and in the two where it was lowest — earnings were between 97 and 101 per cent of costs.[12] It is also noteworthy that the West European airlines have lost money on the North Atlantic, where traffic is very heavy, and made it on their African routes where it is more sparse.

It could be argued that whatever has happened in the past, regulation will make it possible for the airlines to engage in beneficial cross-subsidization in future. It is doubtful, however, whether the gains from increasing the frequency of service are very large and there is reason to believe that such gains will be achieved even when airlines are not protected against competition. On long-haul routes more frequent flights will often have relatively little impact on inconvenience time. Curfews at airports together with international time differences impose severe restrictions on the times at which aircraft are able to depart. At Heathrow, for example, flights are banned between 23.30 and 06.30. As a result it is impossible for subsonic flights from New York to take off between about 11.30 and 18.30 because if they did they would arrive during the curfew at Heathrow.

Even on short-haul and medium-haul routes where international time differences and airport curfews are of no great significance, increases in frequency have less impact on inconvenience time than may be supposed. This is shown by a study for the Brookings Institution, in Washington, by

George Douglas and James Miller, who estimated the relationship between inconvenience time and the number of flights using data from the domestic market in the United States. According to their formula the average inconvenience time is only one hour and 32 minutes when there is a single flight per day. It then falls by 25 minutes to one hour and seven minutes for two flights and by a further eleven minutes to 56 minutes when the number increases to three. After this, each extra flight leads to a small reduction in inconvenience time and it is no more than three minutes when the seventh flight is added.[13] But this is somewhat misleading because the reduction of three minutes relates to a much larger number of passengers than the initial fall of 25 minutes. If, on the basis of the average figures, one calculates the fall in the total inconvenience time for existing passengers when another flight is introduced, and then divides this by the number of passengers on the additional flight, it is found that the reduction per incremental passenger declines only from 25 minutes when the second flight is added to eighteeen minutes when the seventh flight is introduced. It is this saving in existing inconvenience time per incremental passenger that should, in principle, be taken into account when it is being decided whether to put on another flight.

In order to allow for the saving in inconvenience time, it is necessary to know how much it is worth. It might be thought that inconvenience time should be valued at the average hourly wage rate (or salary rate) of airline passengers. In the case of those who are travelling on company accounts this will, together with employers' social security and similar payments, represent the net benefit which firms derive from their employees' services. And for those who are paying their own fares, the hourly wage rate reflects the value which they place on their time because, after deducting taxes that fall on income, this is the price at which leisure can be exchanged for money. If, however, the inconvenience time of those who are travelling on business is valued at the average wage rate, it is being assumed that such time is completely wasted. This is unrealistic as it may well be possible to re-arrange meetings and other activities in order that some or all of the time can be used productively. Where travel is a leisure activity, it is inappropriate to value inconvenience time at the (adjusted) wage rate of the passengers not only because they may be able to employ some of their time usefully but also because this rate includes compensation for the disutility of labour, as well as for the loss of potential leisure. It therefore seems reasonable to suppose that airline passengers place a relatively low value on inconvenience time.

It will be assumed that inconvenience time is valued on average at a notional 25 per cent of median hourly earnings of professional, technical and administrative workers in the United States, which, in 1981, would have given it a value of $3.28 per hour.[14] The earnings of this group of American workers have been used because they are highly paid and airline users tend to be affluent. The British Department of Transport has concluded, however, on the basis of various studies of surface transport in the United Kingdom, that those who are travelling during their own time value it at about 25 per cent of the average hourly wage rate.[15] A substantial proportion of air passengers travel during company time, but, for them the value of inconvenience time must be smaller than the value of time spent in a surface transport vehicle because the former can often be used for some purpose other than travel. If in accord with the Douglas and Miller formula, there is a reduction of 25 minutes in average inconvenience time per passenger when the number of flights is increased from one to two each day, the original travellers will enjoy an average benefit of $1.38. This should in principle be taken into account when it is decided how many flights to provide. As has been seen, the benefit for the existing passengers should, together with the amount which the incremental passengers are prepared to pay, be compared with the additional costs that are being incurred. The benefit, at $1.38 per passenger, would only be sufficient, for instance, to cover 0.8 per cent of the average cost per passenger, at $165 including capital charges, on those West European routes where frequency is low.[16] The figure of 0.8 per cent would be even lower if initially two or more flights were being provided.

Although these figures are only 'guesstimates', the contribution towards extra costs which passengers might be willing to make appears to be so small that it is difficult to believe that it can, in reality, be very large.[17] And, if the potential contribution is small, it is almost certainly undesirable that airlines should be protected against competition in order that they earn monopoly profits on those routes where frequency is high out of which they can help finance extra flights on those where it is low. In the absence of competition, or the threat of competition, costs are almost bound to be somewhat excessive and, as has been seen, regulation does appear to have led to unnecessarily high levels of expenditure in the aviation industry. Because the benefit which existing passengers derive from additional flights is so small in relation to the *extra* costs involved (and even smaller in relation to total expenditure) it would be extremely surprising if the benefit were not more than matched by the additional costs that result from the banning of competition. Cross-subsidization is therefore likely to reduce welfare and not to increase it.

Hitherto what has not been questioned is the belief that there will come a point where, other things being equal, it is desirable to operate more flights even though it is impossible to cover costs. This means that the case for subsidizing or cross-subsidizing the provision of extra flights on routes where they are infrequent has not yet been wholly demolished: it has merely been argued that the potential benefits are likely to be small and are almost certain to be outweighed by excess costs. One way in which airlines may be able to meet their expenditure when additional flights are provided is (i) by introducing a premium fare for those existing passengers who value their time highly and receive substantial benefits when the service is improved and (ii) by instituting a concessionary fare which is sufficiently low to fill most of the extra capacity that is being provided. Airlines will be able to distinguish roughly between the two groups of passengers in the way that they do at present; that is, by charging more to those who are not prepared to book in advance, stay a minimum length of time or meet some other requirement.

It may be thought that any airline which adopts a discriminatory charging system can be undercut, but this is not the case. If there is initially a break-even situation, discrimination is necessary in order that each flight shall be able to pay its way when frequency is increased. This is because of the assumption that the point has already been reached at which the increase in traffic generated by an extra flight is insufficient at the prevailing fare to fill the additional seats. As the new flight will attract some of the passengers from existing flights, it is unlikely to be profitable unless price discrimination is adopted.

LARGER AEROPLANES AND LOWER COSTS

Another reason why the airline industry's output may be sub-optimal, even if fares are no higher than the break-even level, is that large aeroplanes tend to have lower costs than small aircraft. Hitherto it has been assumed that all aeroplanes are of the same size and have the same unit costs. As was seen previously this is not entirely realistic. Where economies of scale exist, because it is possible to use large, low-cost aeroplanes instead of smaller, high-cost ones, the long-run average cost is falling, although there will not be the smooth and continuous curve of the economic textbooks, because only a limited number of different types of aircraft are available. If the average cost is falling, as it will up to the point where the largest aeroplanes can be used, the marginal cost must also be falling and will be below average cost. As has been seen, resources will only be used with the maximum efficiency if in the long run the price is equal to the long-run marginal cost. If the fare is set equal to the marginal cost and the average cost is above the marginal cost, airlines will make losses. As privately-owned concerns will not be able or willing to bear these losses, this may seem to be an argument in favour of regulation.

What this ignores is that airlines will, under the pressure of competition, be forced to provide discount fares based on their incremental costs. This will be a move towards marginal cost pricing. Assume that initially a uniform charge is being made and that small high-cost aircraft are being used to provide a frequent service. The cost of carrying extra passengers will be the amount by which the cost of operating a large aeroplane exceeds the cost of using a small one. Some enterprising airline will therefore decide to introduce a system of differential charges. There will be discount fares which are subject to some kind of restriction and based on the average incremental cost. These will largely be purchased by new passengers. In addition, there will be premium fares which will be paid by existing passengers — those who are not prepared to book ahead, stay a minimum time or meet some other condition. The premium fare will be similar to the uniform charge which airlines were using initially, equivalent to the long-run average cost of providing the existing service with relatively small high-cost aeroplanes.

This may seem unfair and to discriminate against those who buy the premium tickets. But the reason why they have to pay a relatively high fare is that they require a frequent service which, because the demand for this is not sufficiently strong, would involve the use of small, high-cost planes. If they did not need such a frequent service the airline would, presumably, have already reduced frequency and concentrated traffic into large, low-cost aircraft. Only where this has happened, or in those markets where traffic is so dense that an airline could charge a uniform fare and maintain a frequent service with large aircraft, can differential fares be regarded as discriminatory. It is only here that they are not cost-based and do not represent a legitimate way of dealing with the problem of declining long-run marginal costs.

Where differential fares are not cost-based, any airline that has them will be open to competitive challenge. Imagine a route where there is, other things being equal, no case for differential fares because the marginal cost is the same as the average cost, at £100 per seat. The incumbent airline, however, is practising price discrimination and charges a premium fare of £150 and a discount fare of £50. If 1,000 passengers pay the premium fare and 1,000 travel on discount tickets, the airline will, even if all its seats are filled, only break even. It will, nevertheless, be almost inviting another carrier to enter. If an entrant (i) charges a premium fare of, say, £100 and obtains all the incumbent's premium traffic and (ii) matches the existing discount fare and obtains half the discount traffic, it will make a loss of £62,500.[18] The incumbent, however, will sustain a deficit of £162,500![19] The obvious way for the incumbent to discourage another airline from entering, and so prevent large losses, is to end price discrimination and to charge a uniform fare. Hence there is no need for regulation either to prevent differential fares, since under competition they are unlikely to be discriminatory, or to enable differential fare schemes to survive. If they are based on costs they will not require any protection.

In spite of the obvious attraction of differential fares, it may be questioned whether they provide the full benefits of marginal cost pricing, as discount passengers are being charged the average incremental cost. The answer is that if differential fares enable the largest and lowest-cost aircraft to be used, the marginal and average cost will amount to the same thing. If, however, the largest available aeroplanes cannot be employed, it would in theory be possible to bring about a further increase in welfare by adopting full marginal cost pricing. This would require the payment of extensive subsidies to the airline industry and could not be brought about through regulation alone. There would be no point, for instance, in affording airlines protection, so that they could with impunity raise their fares above their average (and marginal) costs on some routes, in order to generate super-normal profits out of which they could then meet the losses incurred on other routes, where fares had been reduced below average costs (and marginal costs).

It seems very doubtful whether in practice it is desirable to subsidize air transport in the name of marginal-cost pricing. All too often subsidies lead to inefficiency, or get put into the pay packets of employees. Moreover, civil aviation is an undeserving industry because subsidies would be likely to have an unfavourable effect on the distribution of income. The poor do not travel by air. It therefore seems best to rest content with the average incremental pricing which should emerge under competition and which has sometimes been frowned upon under regulation.

NOTES AND REFERENCES

1. *Civil Aviation in Europe*, *op. cit.*, p. 61.

2. ICAO Circular No. 180-AT/169, *op. cit.*, p. 10.

3. *Regulatory Reform: Report of the CAB Special Staff*, *op. cit.*, pp. 102-07; and Straszheim, *op. cit.*; pp. 91-96.

4. Graham and Kaplan, *Competition and the Airlines: an Evaluation of Deregulation*, *op. cit.*, pp. 108, 211 and 212.

5. *Stock Research: Airlines*, Salomon Brothers, New York, 24 September 1984.

6. Graham and Kaplan, *Competition and the Airlines: an Evaluation of Deregulation*, *op. cit.*, p. 80.

7. Nulty, *op. cit.*, pp. 127 and 134.

8. Graham and Kaplan, *Competition and the Airlines: an Evaluation of Deregulation*, *op. cit.*, pp. 210 and 213-14.

9. Here and elsewhere capacity is to be thought of as excluding those seats which are required in order that airlines can, in spite of random surges in traffic, provide seats. The desirable load factor is being regarded as fixed and known and the problem of what it should be is ignored.

10. Those with some knowledge of economics may find a diagram helpful. There is a service from A to B with one aeroplane per day in each direction. The demand curve for this level of service is D_1. The avoidable cost per passenger is very low, along AB, until the aeroplanes become full when the short-run marginal cost becomes infinite through E. It will be assumed that the airline is in long-run equilibrium and hence, when it charges the (rationing) fare F_1, it earns a surplus ($ABEF_1$) over and above its avoidable costs which is just equal to its fixed costs.

If the airline were now to employ two more aeroplanes of the same size, the amount of capacity would double from C_1 to C_2 and, in the absence of any economies of scale, the short-run marginal cost curve would shift along and over to BGH. The improved level of service because of the new flights might conceivably shift the demand curve from D_1 to D_2 This would mean that the airline would, at a fare of F_1, earn an extra surplus (BGHE) that would cover its additional fixed costs.

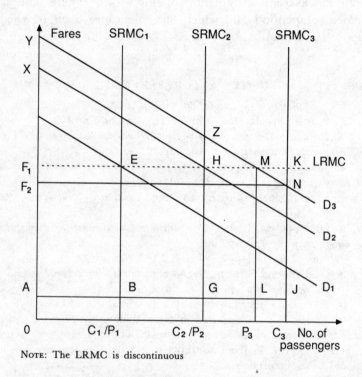

NOTE: The LRMC is discontinuous

It is, however, unrealistic to suppose that an increase in frequency will continue to lead to a proportionate rise in demand. Let it therefore be supposed that if the airline puts on two more aeroplanes the demand curve will only shift to D_3. As the short-run marginal cost curve will move along and over to GIK, the airline will fail to cover its incremental fixed costs (GIKH) if it continues to charge F_1. Traffic will only increase from J_2 to J_3, the additional net revenue will only be GLMH and the airline will incur a loss of

LIKM. Moreover, in order to fill its available capacity (at C_3), and so maximize economic welfare, the airline should reduce its fares to F_2. If so, it will have a deficit of $F_2 NKF_1$.

Nevertheless, it is clearly desirable that the fifth and sixth aeroplanes should be employed. The additional amount, XHC_2C_3NY, which consumers are prepared to pay when they are introduced and the optimal fare is charged, is greater than the incremental costs at C_2C_3KH.

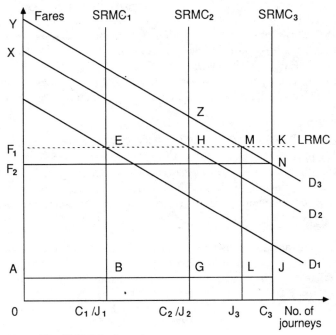

NOTE: The LMRC is discontinuous

What appears to make aviation (and other public transport) distinctive is that when output is increased existing users enjoy a benefit even at the existing level of fares. Thus, when the fifth and sixth aeroplanes are put on, their consumer surplus rises by $XHZY$ (and the benefit HMZ enjoyed by new customers, when F_1 is charged, must also be taken into account). It may be replied that existing users enjoy a gain in consumer surplus whenever a firm makes an improvement in quality. It is usually possible, however,

for producers to adjust their capacity and output up to the point
where the price is equal to the long-run marginal cost. In terms
of this diagram this would mean expanding capacity to at least J_3
where the highest demand curve intersects F_1, which would then
be equal to the long-run marginal cost. But in the aviation industry
(and other forms of transport) it may be impossible, or expensive,
to make small increases in capacity and frequency because of
indivisibilities and economies of scale. For the present, though, it
is assumed that only one type of aircraft is available.

11. See the previous footnote, especially its last paragraph.

12. *Air Fares in Europe: Update of the 1979 Study*, *op. cit.*, p. 12.

13.   Christopher C. Findlay, 'The Optimality of Competitive Air
Transport Markets: a Review of Aspects of the ICAP Report',
Economic Record, Melbourne, June 1982, p. 150.

14. *Statistical Abstract of the United States: 1984* (Washington: Bureau
of the Census, United States Department of Commerce, 1983) p.
434.

15. *Report of the Advisory Committee on Trunk Road Assessment
Chairman, Sir George Leitch* (London: Her Majesty's Stationery Office,
1977) p. 20.

16. *Air Fares in Europe: Update of the 1979 Study.*, *op. cit.*, p. 12.

17. In principle, it is also necessary to take into account the
benefit (or disbenefit) because the amount that additional passengers
are prepared to pay exceeds (or falls short of) the costs of putting
on another flight.

18. The airline's costs will be £200,000 (2,000 seats at £100 each),
its revenue from premium passengers will be £100,000 (1,000
passengers at £100 each) and its revenue from discount passengers
will be £37,500 (500 passengers at £75 each).

19. The airline's costs will be £200,000 and its revenue from
discount passengers will be £37,500.

Chapter 5

Arguments Summarized and Progress Assessed

THE previous three chapters have examined the general and theoretical arguments against liberalization, the American experience of de-regulation and the performance of the international airline system which, because of restrictive agreements between carriers and countries, is only weakly competitive. A large amount of ground has been covered and, of necessity, a considerable amount of somewhat indigestible material has been presented. It therefore seems desirable to provide a fairly extensive conspectus bringing together theory from Chapter 4 and practice from Chapters 2 and 3.

ARGUMENTS FOR REGULATION ARE
UNCONVINCING

Those who believe that the civil aviation industry should be regulated think that because the cost of carrying an additional passenger will generally be negligible, competition will inevitably result in destructive price wars. This, however, pre-supposes that there is capacity available over and above that which airlines plan for so that they may be able to meet random fluctuations in demand. If airlines were to make a substantial reduction in fares, there would often be occasions when travellers would be unable to obtain seats on the flight of their choice. Some of them would then be prepared to pay a premium, as they do at present, so that they could travel on the most convenient flight. If excessive capacity is provided, competition will drive fares down and fixed costs will not be covered in full. Airlines, however, will only acquire aircraft so long as the prospective increase in revenue is at least sufficient to cover the estimated increase in costs, including capital charges. There does not seem to be any good reason why demand in the aviation industry should be particularly difficult to forecast or, even if it is, why predictions should tend to be on the high side.

It is true that in the United States, where de-regulation has taken place, the industry incurred losses between 1981 and 1983 and Braniff was forced to close down. But its collapse was reported to be caused by gross mismanagement and the industry's financial difficulties were due to the recession and the huge rise in oil prices in 1973. Although the short-haul carriers were profitable, other operators lost heavily because, as a result of regulation, they possessed too many wide-bodied jets and consequently price wars developed in long-haul markets. De-regulation meant that, instead of fares being maintained at a time of excess capacity, they were reduced and the load factor remained high by American standards. The greater flexibility of international fares has also had a favourable effect on the utilization of capacity.

The maintenance or increase in fares when excess capacity emerges may have a beneficial short-term impact on the profitability of airlines, but it will mean that seats that might have been filled remain empty. This is likely to be the situation when airlines have a cartel arrangement and there is an inevitable waste of resources. Moreover, airlines will have little incentive to make realistic forecasts of demand if they know that, instead of having to bear the consequences of excess capacity, they will be able to maintain or increase their fares. When regulation has been strict, load factors have tended to be low and, in spite of high fares, profitability has been poor.

The second main argument against liberalization is that the industry is inherently monopolistic. This is at variance with the first argument which assumes that in the absence of regulation there will be too much competition. Moreover, if there are large economies of scale the bilateral agreements between countries stand condemned because, instead of consolidating traffic, they divide it between the national operators. In fact size *per se* does not appear to be of any great advantage in aviation. In the United States, the traffic share of the trunk carriers has fallen from 88 per cent in 1978 to 75 per cent in 1984. It would, however, be wrong to attach too much significance to this because in 1978 the big airlines were inefficient as a consequence of regulation. They are now improving their operating efficiency and, instead of giving ground, are starting to re-capture their original market share.

What is helpful is for an airline to have a well-devised network — a hub airport with radiating spokes — and to account for a high proportion of the flights on any given route. But, although a hub-and-spoke system with its connecting flights will tend to raise load factors, it will generally lead to longer turn-around times and depress aircraft utilization. Moreover, an operator providing a service from A to B via C will be open to competition from an airline which provides one via D or, if the volume of traffic is sufficient, introduces direct flights. Carriers are now competing in both ways in the United States where, since de-regulation, the airlines have been building better hub-and-spoke systems. And, in spite of the advantage to one operator of providing a high proportion of flights on any one route, there has, in fact, been a substantial increase in the number of operators per route in the United States of America. Carriers seem to be willing to operate on routes where they only account for a minority of flights because of the feed traffic involved and the consequent improvement in load factors elsewhere.

Entry into the aviation industry should be relatively easy. Because secondhand aircraft can be purchased, no great amount of capital is required and, since aircraft can be transferred from route to route, existing operators will be reluctant to reduce their prices to short-run marginal costs in the way that they would if their assets had no alternative use. That entry is not difficult is suggested by the American experience. Between 1978 and 1983 the major airlines that were in existence at the beginning of the period ceased to operate on 60 per cent of their old routes but introduced services on an equivalent proportion of new routes. This is an impressive figure, even though the period since de-regulation has been an exceptional one. By 1984 new airlines, together with former charter and intra-state carriers, had succeeded in building up a market share of 10 per cent and most of them have been engaged on large-scale expansion. Not all of the new airlines are financially secure so they may not all manage to become established. Other airlines, however, are joining their ranks or adopting their tactics.

Although traffic is insufficient to support more than one or two operators on many American and international routes, ease of entry suggests that most markets can readily be contested. This, to quote Elizabeth Bailey (a former member of the CAB) and John Panzar of Bell Laboratories, means that 'even if actually operated by only a single firm, their performance should approach the competitive norm, at least to a tolerable approximation.'[1] The American experience since de-regulation suggests that this is the case. According to investigations by staff members of the CAB, fares in monopoly markets are no more than 12 per cent higher than those where the degree of concentration is exceptionally low and the premium of 12 per cent may well decline as competition increases. Moreover, the most appropriate comparison would seem to be that between monopoly routes and those where concentration was about average. This is because the general level of fares appears to be at competitive rather than monopoly levels. Between 1977 and 1983 the real revenue per passenger-mile fell by 14 per cent whereas the regulatory fare level remained about the same in real terms (see Chapter 3).

The final major argument against a policy of *laissez-faire* in the aviation industry is that, even in the absence of monopoly pricing, output will not be expanded sufficiently. The provision of more flights on a route will, unless they are already very frequent, make the service more convenient and existing passengers will be prepared to pay more. This should in principle be taken into account when deciding whether to put on a further flight. It is desirable that the extra amount that existing passengers are willing to contribute, together with the sum that additional passengers are prepared to pay, should exceed the additional expenditure involved. This holds good even if the traffic generated by the improved level of service is insufficient for all (not just the additional) costs to be covered when fares are reduced to the level necessary to fill, and not waste, the available capacity. Although this is really an argument for government financial support, airlines that are protected could in theory practice cross-subsidization and provide extra flights where they are infrequent and existing passengers may receive large benefits.

There is, however, no reason to believe that this is what happens in practice: there is no clear tendency for West European routes to become more profitable as traffic and frequency of flights increase. On long-haul routes airport curfews and international time differences impose restrictions on the timing of flights, and it appears that on short-haul and medium-haul routes higher frequency leads to a surprisingly small reduction in the gap between the time that passengers would ideally like to travel and the time of the scheduled services, even on routes where frequency is low to begin with. Moreover, it seems unlikely that airline passengers, in spite of their affluence, place a high value on the frequency of their services because it will often be possible to re-arrange meetings and activities so that some or all of their time can be used productively. Back-of-an-envelope calculations suggest that the average value which existing passengers derive from an extra flight on a low-frequency service is likely to be small in relation to the average fares they pay. Hence it would be surprising if the gains from cross-subsidization and greater frequency on low-density routes were not more than matched by the excess costs which will develop when airlines are protected from competition. Finally, airlines will be able to recover their costs when they put on extra flights by charging their existing passengers a premium fare and their new passengers a concessionary price. Where airlines would have to use small high-cost planes in order to provide a frequent service, they will again be able to employ differential pricing and introduce discount fares based on the low incremental costs of flying large aircraft instead of small ones.

THREE ARGUMENTS FOR LIBERALIZATION

De-regulation shows that, in practice, competition tends to improve the service available to airline users by extending their range of choice. People Express and other new operators now provide a very cheap, no-frills service and/or are based at secondary airports. The option of rock-bottom fares, and supplementary charges for all discretionary facilities, is one that has until recently been denied to international travellers. The only place where it exists is on the People Express trans-Atlantic route. One of the great disadvantages of the monopolistic arrangements in international aviation is that they inhibit innovation. It is notable that where marketing developments have taken place they have been set in train by outside competition from the charter operators.

The second and most serious weakness of regulation is that, because the discipline of competition is absent or reduced, unit costs are unnecessarily great. In the United States, under regulation, restrictive work-rules depressed productivity and and the pay of airline workers was pushed up to an excessively high level compared to workers in other industries. Some of the new entrants have substantially lower costs than the traditional carriers and this is only partly due to the provision of a no-frills service. Airlines outside North America, however, generally have high costs even by the unexacting standards , of that continent. After allowing for differences in input prices and the length of haul, unit costs are *substantially* greater for international services within Western Europe, Africa and the Middle East than for international services within North America; in Central and South America and Asia and the West Pacific, unit costs are *significantly* greater. On international routes where North American airlines fly, (adjusted) unit costs tend to be low, and wherever West European, African and Middle Eastern carriers operate they tend to be high. Unit costs (after adjustment) are significantly greater for the services of West European airlines outside Western Europe than they are for the international routes operated by the major airlines in the United States. The (adjusted) unit costs of the West European operators are substantially higher for their West European services than for the domestic services of airlines in the United States. It is also significant that where detailed comparisons have been made between West European charter and scheduled carriers, the latter turn out to have greater costs (Chapter 2).

Unproductive use of staff and equipment is almost certainly the main reason why West European and other airlines have such high costs. A subsidiary explanation is that, after allowing for general differences in pay, the remuneration of pilots and cabin staff is higher at most West European airlines than in the United States, even though it appears to be excessive there too. Crews also seem to be highly paid at airlines owned by middle-income countries. Although there may be a tendency for the relative pay of West European ticketing and sales staff to be excessive by American standards, it is probably less marked.

In the United States, competition is now leading to a reduction in real unit costs. Between 1979 and 1984 they appear to have fallen substantially faster than during the period prior to de-regulation and the effort to cut costs has been gaining momentum. During 1983 and 1984 most of the major airlines obtained important productivity concessions from their staff and at a number of carriers, inflated levels of pay have been cut.

The third main weakness of the international aviation industry is that fares are not adjusted at all closely to costs and the amount of capacity is not at all closely matched to the demand. This is shown by the variations in profitability which exist and persist. There are significant differences in profitability between regions and route groups; there are substantial variations between the airlines that operate within each route group; and, when the industry is broken down by airline within route group, the variation in profitability is huge and in only a small minority of the airline sectors are revenue and expenditure roughly balanced. As this suggests, international carriers engage in extensive cross-subsidization.

In Western Europe, at least, there is a poor relationship between prices and costs for different types of fare. Standard fares tend to be above and discount fares tend to be below costs. This is because the airlines engage in price discrimination and raise fares where demand is insensitive to price and reduce them where it is price-sensitive. It seems likely that there is also some discrimination in the United States although, as a result of competition, discount fares there are now so readily available that only about one fifth of all passengers pay the full fare, as against 50 per cent in Europe.

INEVITABILITY OF DE-REGULATION

In spite of the strength of the case in favour of liberalization, governments remain for the most part strongly committed to regulation. The idea has become deeply ingrained that, because they possess sovereignty over their air space, the right to operate air services should be jealously guarded. It does not, however, follow that because a government possesses sovereignty it should use it to protect national firms and to prevent competition. But this *non-sequitur* has, through constant repetition and long habit, become extremely powerful. Moreover, many governments fear that if regulation were to come to an end their national carriers would lose ground because of their high costs.

Nevertheless, it would be wrong to conclude that regulation will last for ever. The Common Market could provide an impetus for reform. The Commission of the European Community is now pressing the Council of Ministers to make a number of changes. In its document, *Progress Towards the Development of a Community Air Transport Policy*, the Commission has proposed

(a) that the governments of the countries at the end of air routes should establish upper and lower limits for fares;

(b) that in the event of disagreement the government of the country of origin should be able to approve the fare in question;

(c) that governments should not be able to insist on their airline (or airlines) obtaining more than a quarter of the total traffic;

(d) that the pooling of revenue should, in effect, be discontinued because no airline should have to transfer more than one per cent of a route's earnings to another operator;

(e) that charter carriers should be able to sell up to around 15 per cent of their seats to those purchasing pure transport and not travelling on inclusive tours; and

(f) that subsidies to airlines should be subject to the Treaty of Rome, which would rule out subsidies to cover operating losses, unless these subsidies are part of a programme of adjustment that would not transfer the problem to other countries.[2]

These would be welcome changes. They would make it somewhat easier for airlines to reduce their fares. An airline that offered reduced fares, however, would need to have the support of its own government and would nevertheless face the difficulty that, unless the other country also wanted a reduction in fares, it would only apply in one direction. If the 'receiving' country was unwilling to allow its airlines to reduce fares *pari passu*, this would mean that an airline which simultaneously cut its outward-bound fares and increased its capacity (or refrained from reducing it at a time of low demand) might not be able to sell all its seats on the return flights. Moreover, because the proposed reforms do not include greater freedom of entry, the two flag-carrying airlines on any route would have no great incentive to behave in a more competitive manner. The only development that would make the position of the existing carriers less secure is the provision that charter operators can enter the scheduled market. The extent to which this would be permitted is likely, however, to be extremely limited.

Hitherto the Council of Ministers has made virtually no progress towards implementing the Commission's proposals, although they were put forward as long ago as March 1984. The Commission threatened that unless action were to be taken by June 1986, it would institute proceedings in the European Court of Justice in Luxembourg and thereby force governments and airlines to take account of the competition rules in the Treaty of Rome. At its meeting at the beginning of June the Commission failed to make any progress and it may therefore proceed with its case, which is under active preparation.

The European Court has just delivered an important verdict on civil aviation. The case began in the civil courts in Paris. Various travel agents were sued for selling Air France tickets at a discount. The magistrate decided that this was too weighty a matter for him and handed the matter over to the European Court. In May 1986 the Court ruled that the competition clauses of the Treaty of Rome applied to air transport. This has opened the way for further litigation and enables those governments who favour greater liberalization to establish machinery to determine whether the restrictive arrangements of the airlines that operate in and out of their countries are violating the competition clauses. The British Government has announced that it is studying the machinery and procedures that would be necessary in order to apply the competition rules. In the end there are likely to be disputes between the authorities in different countries about whether (i) the restrictive arrangements of the airlines are incompatible with the Treaty of Rome which in Article 85(1) prohibits price fixing, capacity restriction and market sharing, or (ii) whether the airlines' arrangements are permissible because, in the words of Article 85(3), they 'contribute to the improvement of the production or distribution of goods'. Ultimately these disputes are likely to be ruled on by the European Court, although it may be a considerable time before they arise.

The Commission of the European Community and the European Court of Justice are not the only possible routes by which progress towards de-regulation may occur. A little progress has now been made towards liberalizing the restrictive bilateral arrangements which govern civil aviation. Since June 1984 the United Kingdom has concluded agreements with the Benelux countries which:

(a) contain no limitations on capacity or frequency of services among these countries;

(b) give either government the right to permit additional airlines to operate on any route;

(c) enable airlines to set whatever fares they choose, unless both governments disapprove.

Arrangements that are less liberal, but nevertheless represent some advance, have also been made between the United Kingdom and West Germany and the United Kingdom and Switzerland. Another important development, and the only one which does not involve the United Kingdom, is the agreement that was made in the Summer of 1985 between the United States and Japan. This provides for more than one carrier from each country on three trans-Pacific routes. Provision was, however, made for a limitation on the number of flights if the governments believe that competition is excessive.

Although these agreements represent only a small breach in the wall that protects the scheduled international airlines from the pressure of competition, their importance should not be under-estimated. They, like de-regulation in the United States, will give rise to working examples of competition in action. It is these examples which will mean that sooner or later, by one route or another, regulation will crumble and liberalization will triumph over much of the world.

REFERENCES

1. Bailey and Panzar, *op. cit.*, p. 129.
2. Civil Aviation Memorandum No. 2, *Progress Towards the Development of a Community Air Transport Policy*, *op. cit.*

List of References

THIS list contains only the more important references cited in the text and additional further readings. The reader should refer to the Notes and References at the end of each chapter for more complete bibliographical information.

DOUGLAS A. ADKINS, Martha J. Langelan and J.M. Trojanowski; *Is Competition Workable in the North Atlantic Airline Markets?* (Washington: International Economics Analysis Group, Bureau of International Aviation, Civil Aeronautics Board, 1982).

ELIZABETH E. BAILEY and DAVID R. GRAHAM, *Deregulating the Airlines* (Boston: MIT Press, 1985).

ELIZABETH E. BAILEY and JOHN C. PANZER, 'The Contestability of Airline Markets During the Transition to Deregulation', *Law and Contemporary Problems*, Durham, North Carolina, Winter 1981.

RIGAS DOGANIS, *Flying Off Course: the Economics of International Airlines* (London: Allen and Unwin, 1985).

CHRISTOPHER C. FINDLAY and PETER J. FORSYTH, *Competitiveness in Internationally Traded Services: the Case of Air Transport*, ASEAN-Australia Working Paper No. 10 (Canberra: ASEAN-Australia Joint Research Project, Research School of Pacific Studies, Australian National University, 1984).

CHRISTOPHER C. FINDLAY, 'Optimal Air Fares and Flight Frequency and Market Results', *Journal of Transport Economics and Policy*, Bath, January 1983.

CHRISTOPHER C. FINDLAY, 'The Optimality of Competitive Air Transport Markets: a Review of Aspects of the ICAP Report', *Economic Record*, Melbourne, June 1982.

PETER J. FORSYTH, *US Airline Deregulation: an Interim Assessment*, Working Paper No. 29 (London: Institute for Fiscal Studies, 1981).

JOSE A. GOMEZ-IBANEZ, CLINTON V. OSTER and DON H. PICKERELL, 'Airline Financial Performance Under Deregulation', Mimeograph.

DAVID R. GRAHAM and DANIEL P. KAPLAN, *Competition and the Airlines: an Evaluation of Deregulation* (Washington: Office of Economic Analysis, Civil Aeronautics Board, 1982).

DAVID R. GRAHAM and DAVID P. KAPLAN, 'Airline Deregulation is Working', *Regulation*, Washington, May/June 1982.

DAVID R. GRAHAM and DANIEL P. KAPLAN, 'Efficiency and Competition in the Airline Industry' *Bell Journal of Economics*, Hickville, New York, Spring 1983.

JOHN R. MEYER and CLINTON V. OSTER JR, with MARRI CLIPPINGER, ANDREW McKEY, DON H. PICKERELL, JOHN STRONG and C. KURT ZORN, *Deregulation and the New Airline Entrepreneurs* (Cambridge, Massachusetts, and London: MIT Press, 1984).

JOHN R. MEYER; CLINTON V. OSTER (eds), *Airline Deregulation: the Early Experience* (Boston: Auburn House, 1981).

ANTHONY SAMPSON, *Empires of the Sky: the Politics, Contests and Cartels of World Airlines* (London: Hodder and Stoughton, 1984).

DAVID STARKIE and MARGARET STARRS, 'Contestability and Sustainability in Regional Airline Markets', *Economic Record*, Barwood, Victoria, September 1984.

MAHLON R. STRAZHEIM, *The International Airline Industry*, (Washington: Brookings Institution, 1969).

Official Publications

Air Fares in Europe (Brussels: Association of European Airlines 1977).

Airfares in Europe: Update of the 1979 Study, AEA/517 (Brusscls: Association of European Airlines, 1982).

Civil Aviation in Europe (Brussels: Association of European Airlines, 1983).

Civil Aviation Memorandum No. 2, Progress Towards the Development of a Community Air Transport Policy, COM(84)72 final (Brussels: Commission of the European Community, 1981).

A Comparison Between European and United States Fares, CAA Paper 83006 (London: Civil Aviation Authority, 1983).

The Changing Airline Industry: a Status Report Through 1982 (Washington: General Accounting Office, 1983), Appendix

Deregulation of Air Transport: a Perspective on the Experience in the United States, CAA Paper 84009 (London: Civil Aviation Authority, 1984).

European Air Fares: A Discussion Document (London: Civil Aviation Conference, 1982).

Regional Differences in Fares, Rates and Costs for International Air Transport 1981, Circular 180-AT/69 (Montreal: International Civil Aviation Organization, 1983).

Regulatory Reform: Report of the CAB Staff (Washington: Civil Aeronautics Board, 1975).

Report of the Advisory Committee on Trunk Road Assessment Chairman, Sir George Leitch (London: Her Majesty's Stationery Office, 1977).

Report on Competition in Intra-European Air Services (Paris: European Civil Aviation Conference, 1982).

Report on Intra-European Air Fares, (Paris: European Civil Aviation Conference, 1981).

A Review of the Economic Situation of Air Transport 1972-1982.

Scheduled Passengers Air Fares in the EEC (Brussels: Commission of the European Communities, 1981) Annex 2.

Scheduled Passenger Air Fares in the EEC, COM(81)398 final (Brussels: Commission of the European Community, 1981).

Survey of International Air Transport Fares and Rates, September 1982, Circular 176-AT/66.

List of Thames Essays

9 PETER LLOYD, *Anti-dumping Actions and the GATT System* (1977), 59 pp.

10 T.E. JOSLING, *Agriculture in the Tokyo Round Negotiations* (1977), 48 pp.

11 HARALD B. MALMGREN, *International Order for Public Subsidies* (1977), 80 pp.

12 DAVID ROBERTSON, *Fail Safe Systems for Trade Liberalisation* (1977), 80 pp.

13 SIDNEY GOLT, *Developing Countries in the GATT System* (1978), 42 pp.

14 THEODORE HEIDHUES, T.E. JOSLING, CHRISTOPHER RITSON and STEFAN TANGERMANN, *Common Prices and Europe's Farm Policy* (1978), 83 pp.

15 HANS BÖHME, *Restraints on Competition in World Shipping* (1978), *Out of Print.*

16 ROBERT E. HUDEC, *Adjudication of International Trade Disputes* (1978), 95 pp.

17 STUART HARRIS, MARK SALMON and BEN SMITH, *Analysis of Commodity Markets for Policy Purposes* (1978), 91 pp.

18 ROBERT Z. ALIBER, *Stabilising World Monetary Arrangements* (1979), 51 pp.

19 ROBERT L. CARTER and GERARD M. DICKINSON, *Barriers to Trade in Insurance* (1979), *Out of Print.*

20 GEOFFREY SMITH, *Westminster Reform: Learning from Congress* (1979), 59 pp.

21 W.M. CORDEN, *The NIEO Proposals: a Cool Look* (1979). *Out of Print.*

22 ROBERT E. BALDWIN, *Beyond the Tokyo Round Negotiations* (1979), 46 pp.

23 DONALD B. KEESING and MARTIN WOLF, *Textile Quotas against Developing Countries* (1980), 226 pp.